THE MORALITY OF PROFITS

I0479921

INDIA · SINGAPORE · MALAYSIA

Notion Press

No.8, 3rd Cross Street
CIT Colony, Mylapore
Chennai, Tamil Nadu – 600004

First Published by Notion Press 2021
Copyright © Sanjeev Raman 2021
All Rights Reserved.

ISBN 978-1-64983-874-2

THE MORALITY OF PROFITS

BEYOND THE PROFIT APPROACH TO A VALUE AIDED PROGRESSION

SANJEEV RAMAN

INDIA · SINGAPORE · MALAYSIA

INDICACADEMY

Indic Pledge

———◆◆———

- *I celebrate our civilisational identity, continuity & legacy in thought, word and deed.*

- *I believe our indigenous thought has solutions for the global challenges of health, happiness, peace and sustainability.*

- *I shall seek to preserve, protect and promote this heritage and in doing so,*
    - *discover, nurture and harness my potential,*
    - *connect, cooperate and collaborate with fellow seekers,*
    - *advance diversity and inclusivity in the society.*

About Indic Academy

———◆◆———

Indic Academy is a non-traditional 'university' for traditional knowledge. We seek to bring about a global renaissance based on Indic civilizational and indigenous thought. We are pursuing a multidimensional strategy across time, space and cause by establishing centers of excellence, transforming intellectuals and building an ecosystem.

Indic Academy is pleased to support this book.

Dedicated to

My parents who have been my heroes in many ways.

My wife for her constant support,

My daughter, the love of my life,

Gautam, my brother-in-law, who has always guided me in difficult times.

Contents

Section IV: Prachaar

Acknowledgements

This book would not have been possible without the constant guidance and support of Mr Gopal Krishnan who is the Ex Founder MD India, Trafigura. His mentorship has helped in maintaining the flow of the book. His questions triggered the grey matter in my brains to re-assess the concepts and refine them. He also took pain to edit the book. He has been an inspiring person who helped me evolve as a writer.

I would like to thank Admiral G Ashok Kumar, Vice Chief of Naval Staff, Indian Navy for having written the foreword for my book. Although I have worked with him almost 3 decades back, the warmth he displayed in grooming me as well as other junior officers on-board during my watch-keeping days still resonates and motivates me to achieve true leadership.

I want to express my thanks to Mr Subhash Naidu, Director of Pitstop Consultancy Pvt Ltd, for introducing me to Gopal. Subhash is a dear friend and shared valuable inputs in enhancing the book.

Special thanks to my daughter Simran Srivastava. She has just completed her undergraduate program in Psychology. She is the first person to read my book in its rawest form and has given her precious insight as a reader.

My special thanks to Ms Aparna Menon, Legal Consultant. Her efforts in editing the book added more value to the flow. She is an exceptionally good editor, very helpful and forthright in giving her comments, which has further refined the book. Her contribution is invaluable to me.

I would also like to thank Mr VKN Umashankar, an independent consultant and friend, for giving editing inputs and feedback.

I express my sincere thanks to my friend Mr Rajat Ghosh for the photo credits. Rajat is an internationally famed photographer whose works have won laurels worldwide.

I owe my gratitude to my father, Mr AK Srivastava, Past District Governor Lions International and Mr PK Sinha, Ex GM (HR), Hindustan Copper Ltd who have constantly encouraged me during the project and for sharing many anecdotes.

I would like to thank Mr Subramaniam Krishnan, CEO of Two Cents Consulting, a marketing and branding consulting company based in Mumbai, for his guidance during the publication and marketing of this book.

I would like to place on record, my sincere thanks to Mr Nitesh Ranjan, Mr Donald D'Souza, Mr Prashant Achar, Mr Amit Chakraborty, Mr Vijay Shanbag for having accepted to review my book before its launch and offer their comments. Their comments inspire me to work on future projects.

I also thank all my friends who shared various messages in WhatApp, which provided me with ideas to refine the book. Many of the stories in the book are inspired by the videos and forwards in WhatsApp group. It is not possible to provide an accurate acknowledgement since the source is not known. I would like to place on record the appreciation for the works of Sadguru Jaggi Vasudev, Ramakrishna Mission, Brahma Kumaris, Dr Ram Charan and Mr Shiv Khera, many of which I have read and which inspired me to work on this project.

Regardless of the source, I wish to place on record my gratitude to all the people who have contributed to the work although anonymously. I have made every effort to acknowledge and give credit for the material used in the book wherever it is due. If it has been omitted inadvertently, the same will be provided in the future publication as and when it is brought to the notice of the author.

My appreciation is also due to the entire team of Notion Press who worked tirelessly to meet the timeline. The editing team under Ms Susan, the marketing research team under Ms Sharon, design team under Ms Adeline all of whom painstakingly worked to bridge the information gap to deliver the final product. I would also thank Ms Manisha and Mr Vignesh who co-ordinated the entire activity from Notion Press in the publishing of the book.

Finally, I wish to acknowledge that, all that I have gained in my life is due to the strong foundation laid by the Indian Armed Forces and Indian Navy, in particular, early on in my career. The values and principles learnt while in the Indian Armed Forces has provided me with a strong footing to face challenges in life. I shall, forever, be indebted to this fine service.

Foreword

As I see it, an action exemplifies who you are. This holds good for the author of this book, Cdr Sanjeev Raman (Retd). I have had a delightful experience of working with him in the Armed Force. He has always been a man of discipline, whose work ethics has left a remarkable impression, leading him to earn respect from all ranks of officers. It is hence a pleasure, to pen a foreword for his book.

Writing is hard, even for authors who do it all the time, so, let me begin by expressing how meritorious reading this book has been for me. THE MORALITY OF PROFITS has led me to believe that its one to be reckoned to. To be able to write about a relevant topic such as Building a Conscious Organisation entwined with Value Aided Progression (VAP) is a brilliant work of words. I find the book infused with a great balance of technical, business and social ethics. I was wholly immersed in the concept of VAP and it is undoubtedly the foreground of the book.

The author's anecdote as an officer in the Armed Forces is quite interesting, especially where he explains about discipline, morals and principles. These are values that all officers will swear by. Several experiences are very relatable, acting as a window for civilian readers giving them a glance of various challenges faced by an officer.

Another interesting aspect of this book is the extensive examples-excerpts from mythological stories and the morals attached to them. Readers will not only get a grounded understanding of each concept but also learn about the complexities and uncertainties of a leader. Just like a dictionary is a window that opens up a world of words and its meaning for those who seek, similarly, this book can help all – leaders, employers, employees, students or just anyone who seeks to understand the concept of VAP and wish to imbibe it to enhance their professional and personal lives.

In the book, the importance of human behaviour in building a conscious organization also caught my interest. I too share similar thoughts on this aspect. I agree with the author that every organization's foundation is built on the kind of human resource that exists and flourishes under it. Responses to one's work environment, be it direct or indirect can act as a crucial factor. Hence, working towards its development is just as important as profiting from it. It has to be a win-win situation for all.

The book elaborates the importance of money with respect to morality, on how it is acquired. As rightly, pointed out by the author, moral values are an extremely important factor that we officers learn during our training and stick to it for the rest of our lives. Moral courage is what makes us take risks for the welfare of the country and the citizens. Military undoubtedly churns out fine leaders. Ones, who are so trustworthy and inspire such confidence in their judgement that their subordinates are willing to follow their orders even at the risk of their lives. The value system and code of conduct are paramount for us. I applaud the intellect of the author, for he has hemmed all these important values with growth, business and profit, thereby handing out to the readers a result-oriented formula to achieve business sustainability and profitability.

As a reader, I find the book universally applicable and relevant. For the country to grow and develop all business operations, be it small or big, need to flourish. Therefore, I feel that the business operative path shown in this book strikes a neat balance between organizational human behaviour, financial aspects of business and strong leadership at the helm. Sanjeev has intelligently used his professional and personal life experiences very efficiently in the book to elucidate the same. I find it, unquestionably an excellent guide for all those who aim to build a conscious, positive and sustainable organization.

I think Sanjeev is a revolutionary thinker, one who wants the society to benefit, through his book. Only a revolutionary person, with his ideas, can dare to challenge the status quo at the risk of upsetting the mundane order or carrying out business or leading an organization. Practical ideas, morals and value system coupled with operative principles laid out in the book will help many achieve business goals. It will at the same time turn and churn things around for the betterment of society.

I wish Sanjeev great success with this book. May it be an ignitor for generations of thinkers, developers, leaders and students. I strongly recommend the principle of Value Aided Progression, as I believe it to be a blueprint to success. Indeed, the readers will unquestionably find the contents of this book, a continuing journey of learning and achieving success.

Vice Admiral G Ashok Kumar

Vice Chief of Naval Staff

Indian Navy

14th Oct 2020

Prologue

This book is about building a conscious, positive and sustainable organization focusing on creating an individualistic character of the organization. It introduces the concept of **Vichaar Aachaar Prachaar (VAP)** to build a universal leadership model with an intent to lay the foundation for a strong and responsible organizational conscience. The concept of **Vichaar** is about the organizational thought process and culture, which forms its immune system. The concept of **Aachaar** is about the behaviour of the people and the actions, which emanates from the culture both at an individual as well as organizational level. It emphasizes the management of self as well as money. The concept of **Prachaar** is about the leadership required to propagate the organizational philosophy both within the organization as well as to the society at large. It emphasizes the importance of building trust with the community in which the organization operates. I call these three aspects as **Value Aided Progression** (**VAP**) so that organizational ecosystem does not degrade its value system, which is essential for its long-term sustainability.

In today's era of artificial intelligence, creativity and the present situation, which the world is facing due to COVID 19 pandemic, the importance of building trust among community and society, by emphasizing on the core value system, is the need of the hour. It helps the organization in appreciating the importance of VAP so that it continues to retain its ability to provide the desired results in a constantly changing external environment.

The book is meant for business leaders, managers and people in a leadership position in an organization. The book highlights the need to strike a balance between organizational human behaviour, the financial aspects of business and strong leadership at the helm for its sustainability. However, the concept of VAP has universal applicability in our lives. Hence, the book can be read by students as it will help them to restructure their thinking process for effective life management. It is however not a self-help book for emancipation.

The book is divided into four sections.

Section I introduces the concept of Vichaar, Aachaar and Prachaar (**VAP**). It explains the evolution of the business priorities spanning over a hundred years. It further delves on how organizational priorities have triggered various shifts to the present environment, where the focus is on building a good organizational character.

Section II focuses on **Vichaar** which lays the foundation of an organization's vision statement. It highlights the importance of building a good corporate culture. As thoughts ensue from people's mind, it is essential to first understand the self. If you understand self, then you can manage self and contribute effectively.

Section III focuses on **Aachaar.** The concept is two-fold – one dealing with the people and others with the profit.

Section IV focuses on **Prachaar** – the needs for strong leadership which must focus on building trust with the employees as well as society/ community with equal emphasis.

Although each section of the book is interrelated and have concepts that flow from one to the other, they can, however, be read and understood independently too.

Advance Praise for the Book

The Morality of Profits is a breath of fresh air in the crowded space of leadership genre books. The author has used the concepts of Aachaar, Vichaar and Prachaar to take the reader through the ideal progression of an organization to stay relevant in today's complex world. This book offers an alternative to Organizations looking to make themselves sustainable while remaining profitable. The concepts are elucidated through examples ranging from Indian mythology, the armed forces and corporate history making it a compelling read.

Vijay Shanbag,
Executive VP, Capgemini India

I loved Sanjeev's tagline "Culture is the immune system of business". The book expands on this in a very 'desi' way with the concepts of Vichaar, Aachaar, and Prachaar – building organizational cultural environments, consequent behaviour and leadership reinforcements. The dwellings on many major complementary aspects – values and ethics -as well as contradictions – spirit versus letter, is very well articulated with wonderful anecdotes. I am particularly impressed with his insights of transforming organizations from Production centric (TQM) to Customer Centric (TPM). I recommend this book to both to a casual reader as well as Leaders who are embarking on a journey to build a

Cultural identity of their organizations. The intensity is as to be expected of a war veteran.

Amit Chakraborty,
Board Member Aequs Consumer, ex MD & CPO Hasbro Far
East, ex VP and CPO Royal Philips, China

I find Building a Conscious Organization, a very relevant topic as its entwined with the concept of Value Aided Progression (VAP)... a brilliant work of words. A must for any corporates, leaders, management gurus and particularly the younger generation, acting as a guide that helps them to understand the importance of ethics, morality in a corporate environment. The author's anecdotes as an officer in the armed force are quite interesting and makes several experiences very relatable to a person who often goes through the dilemma of making right choices when it comes to achieving an end. The way the examples-excerpts from mythological stories have been infused to buttress the points relating to the importance of values of an organization and its leaders are not only relevant but also makes it a good read. I believe, this book undoubtedly holds content that can kickstart a journey of learning and research for times to come."

Nitesh Ranjan,
General Counsel –Legal, Global Operations Mobileum
Technologies

Amidst the heap of books on a similar subject, what differentiates Morality of Profits is the lucid flow of the complicated topic. The anecdotes make the concept memorable. It is a good work on human behaviour alongside business ethics. An informative read for all genre. In summary, the distilled wisdom of yore is condensed into Aachar, Vichaar and Prachaar! Go ahead, read it... I assure you it's a one-sitting read... and worth it!

Best wishes!

Prashant Achar,
CEO, GP Petroleums

SECTION I – INTRODUCTION

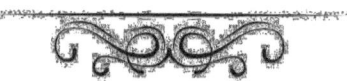

Chapter 1

The Question of Ethics, Values and Culture

1.1 Value Aided Progression – The Aspect of Vichaar, Aachaar and Prachaar

This book, given that no one had any experience in dealing with a pandemic like Covid-19, seeks to chart a path for organisations to future-proof their businesses with an emphasis on values and integrity. Building an individualistic character of the organization to inspire people's conviction and trust in them is the need of the hour. We are living in a complex world which is changing very rapidly. Today, technology has a significant influence on our lives, be it professional or personal. Technology also brings enormous convenience. Smartphones, for example, not only helps in faster business transactions but also provides enormous convenience in doing very many things from the comforts of our homes. Non-availability of the internet is considered to be the biggest disrupter in our life and is now a fundamental right too.

In exchange, the use of technology demands trust from the people applying it in their lives who are expected to share their personal information with unknown faces. At times, this creates a sense of insecurity for the user, when it is misused, abused and exploited. These changing situations, on which we have no control, puts undue pressure on us and even cripples our logical reasoning and decision-making ability. At times, it takes away our ability to respond. Many people are simply unable to handle the situation created by this external surrounding despite their best aptitude and inherent talent. On most occasions, we only have an impulsive reaction.

The Mahabharata – the great Indian epic is a story of a struggle between cousins, The Kauravas and The Pandavas. Prince Arjuna (the third Pandava prince) was the greatest archer of his time and a great warrior. Both Kauravas and Pandavas believed that he was the pivot in this crucial battle. Every strategy of the Kauravas was focused on engaging him because he was considered the key between winning and losing the battle. Arjuna was not only very proud of his achievements and but also had full faith and confidence in his capabilities. But at the start of the battle, when he sees his adversaries against whom he had to fight, he suddenly lost his confidence and self-belief. He was overwhelmed by the external environment and its consequences that he decided to give up the arms. He questioned himself, "What am I going to gain from this battle?" Similarly, we all face such situations in our lives. We have little or no control over the external conditions which have far-reaching influence in our lives. Even though we believe and may have the competence and skill to handle the situation, we often get

confused. Our thought process gets muddled. We either decide to give up or are unable to deliver the desired results. That was when Lord Krishna delivered the teachings of Gita to Arjuna while on the battlefield of Kurukshetra. On hearing the teachings of Gita, which is the spiritual dialogue between Arjuna and Lord Krishna, Arjuna's mind is enlightened. He could think with clarity and recognized the purpose of his life. He understood that to serve humanity in a better way, he had to fight this battle and win. He understood that even though personally one is satisfied with the bare minimum, but if you wish to serve the community at large, you need to follow the Dharma way. The Believer Arjuna turned into an Achiever! He won the battle.

Just like Arjuna, if we want to shift our thought process from just being a Believer to becoming an Achiever, we need to change the focus from "What we want to do" to "Why we want to do it" and more importantly "How we want to do it". In recent years, the "How" component has gained more relevance.

In today's scenario, an organization needs to focus on the triple P (People, Profit and Planet) for its continued sustainability. The book intends to re-create the triple P model to build a conscious and sustainable organization by emphasizing on the following three aspects.

- **Vichaar** – In Hindi literature, Vichaar means the philosophy or your thought process.

- **Aachaar** – In Hindi literature, Aachaar means the behaviour or the actions which emanate from your thoughts.

- **Prachaar** – In Hindi literature, Prachaar means the propagation of philosophy and actions to society.

I call the above-mentioned aspect as Value Aided Progression or simply Vichaar Aachaar Prachaar (**VAP**). The organizational model based on VAP prevents the organization from crossing the tipping point. It helps the organization to retain its ability to continually provide the desired results in a constantly changing external environment.

The first aspect *Vichaar* deals with people's thinking ability. It highlights the importance of organizational philosophy which builds its value system and culture. It emphasizes on the significance of positive thoughts which is the foundation of any progression. It explores your inherent capability and belief to enhance your potential through self-management. It develops and improves your thinking ability. I call this aspect *Vichaar* because it is your thoughts that guide your life and provide insight to meaningfully balance and handle work life. It makes you aware and helps you to discover who you are? What are your strengths and capabilities? What are your limitations, your likes/ dislikes, where you want to be in future and how to achieve it? It enhances your influence on yourself.

"Watch your thoughts; they become words.

Watch your words; they become actions.

Watch your actions; they become habits.

Watch your habits they become character;

Watch your character; it becomes your destiny."

Author unknown

The second aspect *Aachaar* deals with action towards value-based profit generation. All organizations need money for their survival. However, what parameters of money-making do we need to anchor on is equally important. "**How**" money is acquired is equally important than "**How much**". The organization must imbibe a sense of business economics among the people for its sustainability. But, if profit is generated by compromising values, then it will never last long. Organizations which gives prominence to this aspect can create leaders and winners who can ensure its continued existence. As long as an organization makes money, people will throng and stick with it. It is often seen that, if and when an organization is under a scanner for unethical investigation and would like to clear its reputation, the people associated with it will vanish. Rebuilding the organization's credibility will then be a herculean task. That is why the organizational philosophy needs to be translated into action to build a value system which should help people in developing good conduct and character along with a sense of generating money. People must display imbibed values in their action. People who have the responsibility to head the organization should demonstrate high moral courage and integrity. They should develop strong organizational values to be imbibed by the future generation. I call this aspect *Aachaar* because your behaviour and the emanating action is guided by the organizational values.

The third aspect *Prachaar* deals with external and internal environments and its effective communication. We have seen that in recent times, most organization have started to focus not just on profits but also on people and the environment, both internally and externally, for a sustainable operation. Organizations are now emphasizing on the need to build their character. The concentration is on building an internal environment to think creatively. The government has, to some extent, focus on the aspect of the external environment too. It has taken steps by making fulfilment of Corporate Social Responsibility a law. But I feel visibility matters and what you do must also be known to the society. It helps in generating goodwill, which at times is more valuable than profits. This requires leadership which works towards building trust while giving equal emphasis to both Vichaar and Aachaar. I call this *Prachaar* because the propagation and communication of organizational philosophy to society at large through effective leadership helps in building faith, conviction and trust. Only then it can spread and transmit among the masses to generate goodwill.

All organizations need a "Purpose". By organization, I mean a company, a government department, a family, an NGO or any other form of organization. To have a clear understanding of VAP (Value Aided Progression), one needs to decide and define the "Interest" of the organization. The interest of the organization lays the foundation on how the business is governed. Are these governed with more emphasis on developing an organizational culture which gives importance to values and ethics and supports to the weaker section/communities, apart from making money? Are these governed purely by materialistic needs which give more importance to profitability and money? The organizational objectives must always be defined based on "The interest of the organization". These objectives, later on, get converted to strategy, tactics, tasks etc. to achieve the desired results. Objectives may vary from organization to organization as well as from person to person depending on who heads the organization.

Let us evaluate the idea of VAP for a social organization. One of the foundations of the Rotary International is the 4-way Test – This is concerned with the things they say or do. It reads as follows

- Is it the truth?
- Is it fair to all concerned?
- Will it bring goodwill and better friendship?
- Will it be beneficial to all concerned?

In April 2019, the Rotary Foundation Board of Trustees decided to remove the Chair of Board of Trustees since the action taken by him were not in line with the basic fundamental principles of the Rotary International. It does pose a question, "Should a business organization also need to act in the same way?" Every organization must devise ways to weed out things which are not in the interest of the organization or its purpose. It reminds me of the Socrates Story of the Triple Filter Test.

Once Socrates (the famous Greek Philosopher) was visited by an acquaintance. He was very eager to share a juicy gossip about their friend and enquired if he would like to know about it. Socrates replied, "You need to pass the Triple Filter test before you tell me the story".

The first filter is "Truth". Socrates asked, "Have you checked whether, what you are going to tell me is absolutely true?" The man replied, "No, I only heard about it from others but". Socrates interrupted him and asked him to pass the second filter which is "Kindness or Goodness". He asked the second question, "You are not sure about the truthfulness of your statement, but is what you want to say Kind or Good?" The man replied, "No, it is just the opposite". Before he could speak any further, Socrates said, "So, neither what you want to say is true, nor is it good or kind. So, let me put the third filter test which is about Usefulness or Necessity. "Is the information you want to share with me useful or necessary for me to know?" The man replied a little hesitantly, "No". "Well", Socrates replied," If what you want to tell me is neither true, good, kind, useful nor necessary, then please do not say anything at all".

Every organization needs to develop its own triple filter test to find the direction in which the organization needs to be steered.

1.2 The Shift in Organization's Priority – Profit Is Not the Sole Criteria

An article published by CNBC on 19 August 2019 highlights that, CEOs of nearly 200 major US companies have voiced that increasing the shareholder's value is no longer their main objective. A new definition of the *Purpose of a Corporation* was issued, wherein, the purpose of a Corporation is now, no longer considered to be of maximizing profits or to serve the shareholders' interest. Instead, investing in employees, delivering value to customers, dealing ethically with suppliers and supporting external communities are the new goals of these US corporations. They felt that the fundamental changes in economic conditions and failure of the US government to provide lasting solutions have forced society to look at companies for guidance on social and economic issues such as environmental safety, gender and racial equality.

The pillars of any sustainable organization depend on three crucial parameters -

- The people – who are part of the organization.

- The profit – it generates or its ability to generate in future for its continued existence.

- The planet – the utilization of the resource to create and maintain the environment for it to thrive. Only then the business will respond positively and proactively.

A healthy human body requires clean air to breathe and nourishing food for energy. A healthy mind wants pure thoughts to build positivity. Both the body and the mind need a wholesome supply of water to keep the environment hydrated. Any imbalance in the three aspects will affect its longevity. A human body can exist for a while without food but certainly not without air and water, which is crucial for its survival.

From an organizational perspective, earlier profits were considered as air. Profit or money is essential for the survival of any organization and its growth. Organizations have now realized that the environment in which it operates is equally critical for its continued growth. It also needs to develop an ecosystem for the community, both internal and external, which makes its employees a happy workforce and not just a productive workforce. It is the oxygen or the air needed for its progression.

Organizations are now emphasizing on Value Aided Progression (VAP) to cater to the three pillars of People, Profit and Planet. They must develop people, who value its culture, ethos, ethics and help in creating its unique "Character". It is no more about people who are only concerned about profits – by any means.

A culture which breeds creativity, which is more focused on ethical behaviour, emphasizes ethics and values, will unconsciously develop a system where its people are enthusiastic and motivated to contribute. The natural outcome will be a growing profitable business organization, a more responsible successor, a more credible NGO etc.

1.3 Understanding Values, Ethics, Culture & Tradition

Most companies now have a Code of Conduct as their corporate culture initiative. It is the Do's and Don'ts and ethical behaviour expected from their employees. In a family system also, such Do's and Don'ts exist as "behavioural expectation from our children." These are a set of rules – a stepping stone towards building a moral behaviour. But, many a time, the elders themselves do not set the right examples for the younger generation. One can follow all the rules and yet be a devil in life. Hence, rules cannot build character.

In Indian culture, Ramayana – the story of Lord Rama – is one of the greatest epics. It belonged to the period of Treta Yuga, the second of the four Yugas (ages of mankind), as per Hinduism. Lord Rama is considered to be a personification of a person who obeys the rule. Yet his personal life was full of miseries. On the other hand, we have Ravana, the King of Lanka. Ravana kidnapped Sita, wife of Lord Rama. He flouted every rule and demolished every conduct of ethical behaviour. Ravana is personified as "Evil" and Rama as the "Saviour". Today Lord Rama is worshipped by Hindu community as a reincarnation of Lord Vishnu. Ravana's effigy is burnt to symbolize the victory of good over the evil.

We have yet another great epic in Indian culture during the Dwapar Yuga (the third of the four Yugas), The Mahabharata – the story of a struggle between two groups of cousins, The Kauravas and The Pandavas. The battle of Kurukshetra is the fight for succession between the Kauravas and the Pandavas. Lord Krishna delivered the teachings of "Gita" during the battle of Kurukshetra. Mahabharata had a character named Duryodhana, the eldest prince of the Kauravas, who followed every rule but not the spirit of it. On the other hand, we had Lord Krishna, who broke many rules to ensure that the spirit, the character, the moral fabric, the intent, with which the rules were written is always upheld. The dilemma is "whom should we follow?" In Ramayana, the rule follower Lord Rama is worshipped and rule-breaker Ravana is despised. In Mahabharata, the rule breaker Lord Krishna is worshipped and rule-follower Prince Duryodhana is loathed.

Inspired from a talk by Sadguru Jaggi Vasudev

In this context, one needs to understand the basic difference between Values and Ethics. Ethics are guidelines for personal conduct addressing the issue of morality. Values are the guiding principles and ideals. Values help us decide "what is important". It stimulates our thought process. Value system can be defined as a doctrine which guides us in making the right choice. It varies from person to person. No two persons in the same organization or a family follow the same set of principles in life. It is an important aspect of human behaviour, which affects our emotional state of mind. Based on the organizational values, the Ethical Code of Conduct is formulated. Values are the bedrock of any organization and ethics a subset of values. If in an organization, transparency is considered as a value, then every important decision is always discussed, deliberated, shared, opinion sought and then decided. There is no room for dictatorship or autocratic behaviour. It will become an enduring preference for future generations also in the organization.

Let us illustrate the distinction between Values and Ethics with examples of a different organization. In the armed forces, one comes across many a situation, when a particular action may not be morally correct but it is still in alignment with the basic tenets and guiding principles of the Armed Forces Value system. We have recently seen a situation in Kashmir valley in April 2017, when an Indian Army Major tied a stone pelter to his jeep to ensure the safety of the people at a polling booth. He and his team were surrounded by stone pelters. He had to come up with an innovative method to manage this hostile external environment to ensure the safety of the people, whose lives were at risk. He was commended by the Army Chief for his presence of mind. Conversely, many people debated about his actions and even condemned it. For him, it was more of a question of ethical conduct or upholding organizational values of winning a war without firing a bullet. He had to decide "between what was right as opposed to what was important."

Another striking example of upholding the organizational value is the behaviour demonstrated by the employees of the Taj Mahal hotel in Mumbai during the terrorist attack in November 2008. Many hotel employees sacrificed their lives to save guests. The questions that crop up are, is saving the lives of guests at the expense of own, form a part of the employee's duty? The Taj Mahal Hotel was closed for more than a year for renovation work. In such circumstances, is the Taj Mahal hotel management, a Tata Group hotel, duty-bound to pay the salaries of all the employees with all facilities, perks and privileges which may not be in alignment with the employment agreement? However, The Taj Mahal hotel management decided to take care of all the employees with full pay and allowances during the period when the hotel was closed for renovation. What would you call this? An Ethical Code of Conduct or the group's Value System?

Let us examine a family organization. Different families may have different preferences for different reasons. Some may want to invest in a good value system and culture for their children while few may want them to learn business skills, which could enable them to financially aide their respective families. For others, education could be the prime focus. If education is a value for a family, every effort is made to ensure that every child gets a good quality education. When a member gets educated and starts earning, it becomes their moral responsibility to ensure that the rest of the younger siblings also get a similar opportunity. If being an earning member is a value, then how sooner one starts to earn becomes the point of focus. Qualification then does not matter.

In the name of organizational ideology and its value system, people can even be converted into assassins or terrorists. For a terrorist, the question of what is right (which is the basis of their ethical conduct) as well as what is important (which is the basis of the value system) converge to their common belief system which compels them to act in a particular way. It becomes an enduring preference for them.

You pull people with your ideology and make them what you are. The same goes for any business organization. An organizational value does not develop overnight. It takes perseverance and commitment of top leadership. The organization should have a shared vision – which is based on their value system.

A vision statement of any organization is always a projection of its Value System. It is how the organization is perceived and nurtured for the future. Organizational values and vision decide what type of skilled employees are needed, what type of system and processes one wants to develop, because ultimately what one chooses is what one will get in the future.

When all people in the organization have common values, belief, and develop a similar set of attitudes, it translates into the organizational culture. Culture evolves when all people share common values. In Hindi literature, Culture means "*Sanskriti*". It means a stable or improved condition – stability in nature, stability in the way masses think. If it improves, it leads to Progression (Pragati). If it gets distorted, it leads to Destruction (Vikriti). Culture is essentially a concept of sharing common belief, knowledge and tradition. With progression and time, it becomes civilization – *Sanskar or Sabhyata* in Hindi literature.

Traditions are a belief system for a section of people, society, or geographical location. It is nothing but a localized culture. In Hindi literature, Tradition means "*Parampara*". For example, in the Navy, the sailors always salute with their palms turned inwards. The sailor's hand gets dirty while working on the decks. During the British period, when the King/ Queen visited, it was considered inappropriate to show dirty hands while saluting. So, the palms were turned inwards. The tradition continues across all Naval Force around the world. Wearing a particular type of dress during the wedding, eating meals at a specific time during an eclipse, guru shishya relationship (teacher – disciple relationship) etc. are all examples of tradition.

If one creates an environment where positive values and culture thrive, one can build an individualistic character for the organization. The character of the organization reflects the behaviour of its people. Building character is a continuous process. One needs to keep weeding out unwanted elements to mirror the true character of the organization based on its value system. If we can build a positive character of the organization, where people can think creatively, where human minds can innovate, then the organization will remain successful for years to come.

Principles are to people what roots are to trees. Without roots, trees fall when they are thrashed with the winds of the pampas. Without principles, people fall when they are shaken by the gales of existence.

Carlos Reyles, 19th-century Spanish author

1.4 Current Environment

Newspaper and television news are more focused on rape, murder, human rights violations etc. I sometimes wonder if this is the kind of world we are living in? Has it deteriorated so woefully that morality is at its lowest trough? In the last few years, another dimension has started to dominate the news, which has changed the focus of the business environment. It has also affected each one of us at an individual level on the economic front. It has become more relevant today since every person, who holds a smartphone today is "media".

The news that dominated the headlines between the period of September -October 19, projects a very different picture.

Frauds worth Rs 32,000 crore rattle 18 public banks within three months, reveals RTI. In the first quarter of the fiscal, 18 public sector banks were rattled by 2,480 cases of fraud involving a huge sum of Rs 31,898.63 crore – India Today 08 September 19

Regulators, auditors should be held responsible for bank frauds – 17 October 19 Times of India, Anurag Thakur, Minister of State for Finance, Govt. of India

Senior citizen loses Rs 25 lakh to SIM swap fraud – 05th August 19 Times of India

HDIL's father-son promoters arrested in PMC banking fraud – September 2019 Times of India

Laxmi Vilas Bank. Religare Fininvest has accused bank management of misappropriating funds to the

tune of Rs 790 Cr (kept as a fixed deposit) – Sept 2019
Times of India

Business operations are getting adversely affected with such highlights. Individually, we have become more suspicious. Trust level has come down. The focus is now shifting more towards creating a value-based organization which can earn the trust of the people at large. Trust building is being done at all levels and for all types of organization, be it business, government, social or family.

At the business level, financial irregularities and moral improprieties are viewed more seriously with deep-seated implications. If it is against the values of the organization, there could be a job loss or a criminal charge and even imprisonment. Business organizations are becoming less tolerant of corrupt practices aimed solely for increasing the bottom line. They try to fiercely protect the organization's credibility and reputation to ensure that society's conviction in them always remains intact.

At the government level also, an effort is being made to change the perception of its officials and the way work gets done. Many senior government officials were forced to retire early due to their incompetence and their corrupt ways of working.

We are always working to prove our credibility or "Individual Identity". Every department of an organization creates numerous reports to prove their efficiency and their contribution towards profit. Everybody feels that their existence is critical to the organization. We all do this just to prove our identity. We fear our extinction.

In the current environment, organizations are now focusing beyond profitability. It is about bringing credibility and preserving the values of the organization. Reduced profitability doesn't mean that companies cannot endure in the future. But, if values are compromised then in future, people will only tell its tale of past glory. It can perish. Indian history is replete with such examples. Kingdoms have been built emphasizing on righteousness and not by collecting money or looting people.

In Mahabharata, the great Indian epic, Bhisma was blessed with wishful death (He can decide his death). He fought alongside Prince Duryodhana (the eldest Kaurava Prince) for the kingdom of Hastinapur. His loyalty was to the throne. It was not towards the country or the kingdom. Had it been towards the kingdom, he could have easily seen that the kingdom will be more secured under the leadership of King Yudhishthira, the eldest son of King Pandu and cousin of Prince Duryodhana. There were a host of legends on Kauravas side including the likes of Guru Dronacharya, King Karna and many others. King Karna was fighting to prove his loyalty towards his friend Prince Duryodhana. He was fully aware that he is not on the side of righteousness. The Kauravas even refused to give just 05 villages to the Pandavas. Had they done that; the battle could have been avoided. But they refused. Ultimately

all the Kauravas got perished, none survived. The Pandavas, who were considered weaker, won the battle, as they fought for righteousness- "The Dharma".

In the above story, the values were compromised by the Kauravas. They believed that they will win the battle due to the presence of great warriors. They were arrogant, which reflected in their behaviour. Ultimately, the leadership could not deliver. The result was – defeat.

To develop a sustainable business model, a balance in all aspects of Vichaar, Aachaar and Prachaar is necessary. Building a conscious and sustainable organization with an effective economic operation, without compromising on values, will need investment in creating a good corporate culture, understanding of business economics at every level and a good leadership, who are role models not just for the organization but to the society at large.

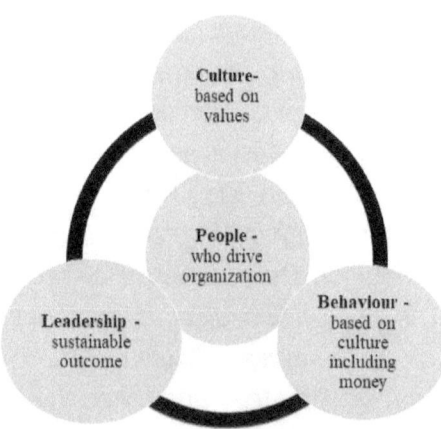

Summary

- *The Interest of the organization should be defined keeping the purpose of the organization in mind.*

- *Values need to be identified and its meaning clarified to enlighten what the organization expects.*

- *Values must give the projection as to how the organization is viewed in future.*

- *Ethical Code of Conduct must be devised keeping the identified values in mind. It needs to be more than just do's and don'ts.*

Action Plan

- It is important to identify the main purpose of the organization. Write the purpose of your organization.

_____

_____

- Recognize the values you want the people in the organization to inculcate.

_____

_____

- Develop your own triple filter test which will separate unwanted information and which can put forth only positive, constructive and valuable thoughts.

_____

_____

- Check your organization's Ethical Code of Conduct. The action it generates must be seen with the intent and the spirit of the values identified – Not just by its ethical merit.

_____

_____

Chapter 2

The Advent of Value Aided Progression – Evolution of Business Priorities

To appreciate the concept of Value Aided Progression (VAP), we must understand the business priority and the leadership concepts that have evolved through the ages with the changing business and social environments.

We have been deeply impacted by rapid advances in technology. Whatever we learn, is constantly becoming outdated. The pace at which technology is advancing is overwhelming. The change is exponential which makes adaptation difficult.

The rapid transforming scenario puts tremendous pressure on the organization's most critical asset – its people. This work pressure affects their social and mental well-being, which is increasingly reflected in their health and happiness. Few organizations have managed to adapt themselves to the pressure of this chaotic transformational change. Those who do adopt the principles of VAP, to overcome this demanding situation which confronts them, finally emerge as leaders. It depends upon the belief system which springs from the culture of the organization. It helps you visualize another perspective.

The Competition

Two hunters were moving around in a jungle when they heard a lion roar. One hunter immediately removed his hunting shoes and put on his running shoes. His friend asked him, "why do you bother to do this and waste precious time? You cannot run faster than the lion." His friend replied, "I only have to run faster than you. The lion only needs one meal to satisfy his hunger." The situation in the corporate world is very much akin to this. You need to be only one space ahead of your competitor, which will give you the time to re-organize. Work pressure affects our social life and vice versa.

From the early 1900s to late 1990- 20th Century

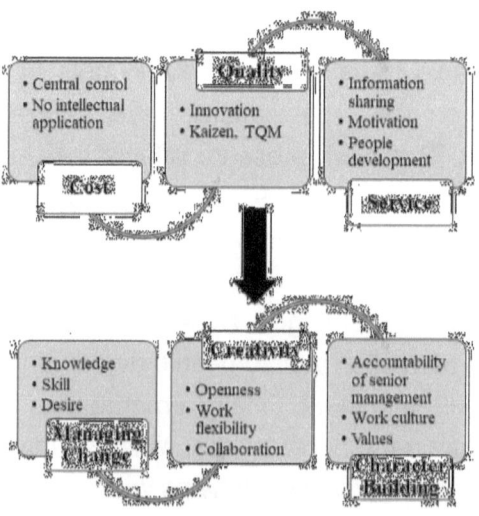

2.1 Early 20th Century – Low Cost and Mass Production – Producer Centric

Centuries ago, groups and individuals functioned through the barter system. Goods produced by one set of people were exchanged for the goods produced by another as well as for the services rendered. After World War I, the first industrial revolution witnessed the development of machines and we slowly moved to the concept of mass production to bring down costs.

"There is one rule for the industrialists and that is: Make the best quality of goods possible at the lowest cost possible, paying the highest wages possible."

Henry Ford

In the early 20th century, Ford Motor Company popularized the concept of mass production. Mass production concept focused on producing items on a large scale to improve productivity and to bring down the cost of production. The age was more producer centric. The focus was always on increasing production through repetitive tasking and not on productivity or quality.

This had a great social impact in improving the quality of life of people as it addressed their physiological needs. We can call this as the American Age because of its origin.

The organization training programs were designed to teach specific job skills related to the concept of "Mass Production". The organizational structure was more pyramidal with centralized command and control.

The authority of the office staff was much high and the workers only followed what was told.

We Have Always Done it This Way

The story is based on a true incident. A consultant was hired by an industrialist to advise him on productivity improvement techniques. During his interaction with the factory staff and scrutinizing the records, he noticed that the quality reports were filled manually in photocopied forms. The form right top corner had faded but people used to be write number "zero" in the box provided on the top right corner. He enquired about the same with many staff who used to fill the report. Nobody could give any satisfactory reply. They just mentioned that they have been writing zero in the box ever since they could recollect. He became inquisitive and visited the record room to get the original form, which was photocopied for the report. When he saw the original form, the mystery got solved. The original form had the mystery box with the heading "Number of Air raids today."

2.2 Mid-20th Century – The Era of Quality Consciousness

With the availability of goods in abundance, the latter part of the 20th century saw a shift in focus on quality using statistical processes. The Japanese were the pioneers in the quality system. The period, post-World

War II, could be called the Japanese Age or the second industrial revolution.

It led to the invention of TQM (Total Quality Management) and other quality assessing tools like 5S, Poko-yoke, kaizen etc. People on the shop floor used innovative ideas to bring change and to improve quality. Japanese industries popularized it more by using the intellectual ability of people. It used the collective intellect of all people on the shop floor to improve quality. The need to be competent, to gain recognition, to know, understand and explore got bigger. The thinking cap was donned by everyone including people on the shop floor. It was no more the domain of the people sitting in the closed-door office.

This age was more customer-centric with focus on providing the customer with a "Choice". It was more of bringing the employees "working hands and minds" to the workplace. Organizations had realized this and were focusing more on TPM (Total People Management).

Sharpening your axe

A woodcutter named Sunny was hired by a timber merchant to cut trees. But even after working for three years, he never got a raise. The company hired another woodcutter, Bill, who got a raise after completing just one year. Sunny complained to his boss. The boss said, "Your productivity over the years has not improved. You are still cutting the same number of trees that you started with." The boss gave him a designated area and asked him to cut the same number of trees as Bill did. Sunny worked with more determination, putting long hours and hitting harder. However, he was unable to meet the standard set by Bill. The boss called Bill and asked, "How did you manage to cut more trees?" Bill replied. "After cutting each tree, I take a break and sharpen my axe. When did Sunny last sharpen his axe?"

"Cost is more important than quality but quality is the best way to reduce cost."

Genechi Taguchi

The Japanese age also focused on creating an environment so that employees could think innovatively. The organization focus was to involve creativity of more and more people and improve individual skills to enhance the quality of the product.

The training programs focused on the creativity and thinking ability of people. Interaction between various divisions increased. People shared their beliefs and passion which in turn improved collaboration, team building and social interaction. The ability to associate with others be it colleagues, friends, family, team members, got a boost. It created a space to connect the workplace more socially, displaying respect for others, in addition to employing their physical and cognitive ability.

2.3 Late 20th Century – Focus on Service Delivery

The third Industrial revolution was led by information technology, which started progressing during the eighties and nineties. The information technology led to the sharing of information. Price and quality were not much of an issue since people had a choice. The focus shifted to customer care and providing quality service. A product's physical appearance and features were important but people also wanted product reliability. The inclination was shifting towards reliability and guarantee. This led to the concept of a Service Level Agreement (SLA).

The service sector was witnessing huge expansion. Branding, service management and quality of service delivery was the need of the hour. New ideas and theories of managing the complete supply chain gained importance.

Creativity – Japanese Fishing Industry

The water close to the Japanese coast did not hold much fish for decades. As the Japanese are very fond of fish, they constructed bigger fishing boats and went further into the sea for fishing. Hence, it started taking them a long time to return from the trip and retain the freshness of the fish. To overcome the problem, the Japanese fishing trawlers installed freezers on-board. This allowed them to stay longer at sea and catch more fish. The love for fish, however, made the Japanese distinguish between fresh and frozen fish. The frozen fish started to sell at a lower price. To tide over the situation, the fishing trawlers built big fish tanks. They would catch more fish and fill inside the tanks. However, due to regular thrashing around, the fish got tired, became dull and lost the fresh-fish taste. The fishing industry was again faced with a crisis.

The Japanese fishing industry came up with an innovative solution to overcome the crisis. To maintain the freshness of fish, they continued to put fish in fishing tanks but with a small shark. The presence of the shark kept the fish constantly on the move. The challenge the fish faced in water kept them alive and fresh.

Similarly, we also need shark-like challenges in our lives to keep us active, alert and energized.

Many hypotheses to measure the quality of service delivery got conceptualized. One of the most successful concepts was SERVQUAL, a five-dimensional method introduced by Valerie Zeithaml, A. Parasuraman and Leonard Berry. Delivering what you promise was the prime focus area. People paid as per the value they perceived from the service and also based on the need to have such a service. Other initiatives like post service rating, mystery shopping, follow up survey etc. also gained significance.

"Although your customers won't love you if you give bad service. Your competitors will."

Kate Zabriskie

The third industrial revolution took much less time. In less than two decades, the use of computers for industrial use started to gain importance. Within ten years, the information technology revolution had transformed the way the industry had worked earlier. The skills required to handle work had undergone an enormous change.

The use of computers increased the speed of work execution and brought in transparency. Organizations started to focus on creating a value system. It was required to constantly balance and improve the workplace environment. This period witnessed rapid development in understanding human capabilities to manage change. The organization gave impetus to self-awareness, self-improvement and self-management. This staged a footing for the aspects of *Vichaar and the first aspect of Aachaar-* building the organizational culture and focus on self-management.

2.4 Managing Change – The Need for Survival

Change management was the foremost requirement to meet the demand of system transparency, collective participation, skill up-gradation and building an organizational culture. It was the fundamental step for any organization's continued existence. Without being able to weather out and efficiently manage change, organizations would have been annihilated in no time. Managing change needs consideration, appreciation and acceptance of the following five Ws and an H :-

- What to Change?
- When to Change?
- Why Change?

- Where to Change?
- Want to Change?
- How to Change?

The anticipation of the problem, grooming and preparing people for the challenges and uncertainties, creating the right environment, and talent retention is key to the success of change management. The change process must address how to eliminate the hindrance associated with the basic element of fear – fear of the unknown, out of control, being outside the comfort zone, inadequate knowledge etc. It must create a sense of growth, learning and satisfaction during the change process.

"It is not the strongest or the most intelligent who will survive but those who can best manage change."

Charles Darwin

Any initiative to change the process stems from IDEA- **I**nformation & **D**ata, **E**xpertise, and **A**spiration. A right balance of understanding of five Ws and an H will help in overcoming the resistance to change.

Information & data provides us with knowledge – about what to change, when to change, where to change and why to change. It is the basic foundation to initiate the change process.

The expertise provides us with the skill sets required to undertake and conclude the change process. It is the stability link for an effective continuation of the change process. It addresses the question of "how to address the change process."

The aspiration is the driving force for the change process. It addresses the question of the need to change – the desired aspect of "Want to change."

If you want to balance the three aspects of IDEA, it needs to work in coordination. If all the three aspects work in isolation, even though there may be a balance, but, the desired outcome will not be achieved. They will always wonder what will be the outcome.

Presence of all characteristics of IDEA is essential for any change to happen. We may know what to change, when to change, why to change and where to change. We may have the skills to address how to implement the change process. But, if there is no desire or motivation of wanting to change, no change can happen. Similarly, even when we have the knowledge and desire but no skill, there will be no change. Even if we have skill and desire, but without knowledge, no change can take place.

Aspiration or desire is always the base or the start point for any change to happen. But, if you push the aspiration to one side, say to gain knowledge and leave the expertise untouched, the seesaw will be tilted. The balance cannot be achieved. Similarly, if the aspiration is focused to gain skill but does not acquire enough information and data about the change process, the balance cannot be achieved. So, how can we achieve an effective change process?

To ensure that the change can take place in the way we expect, the aspiration should create a pull system for both knowledge and expertise. There has to be a desire in each element of IDEA on its own. If the knowledge and the expertise move at the same pace towards the aspiration, all the three can balance at the centre and move ahead together.

The success of the change process is measured by checking how the business outcome responds to the environment it operates. It is considered successful if it responds proactively, productively and effectively. To successfully manage change, two things are very important:

- Making people understand why change is essential for their survival. Unless the benefits are more than the investment in up-gradation of skill and knowledge level, there will be no support to the change process.

- Invoke the inner strength of people to manage self. The desire to change stems from this aspect. Unless we prepare ourselves to operate outside our comfort zone, the change will not happen.

Be the Eagle

The Eagle can live up to 70 years. Although it can withstand harsh conditions outside, to survive, and live up to that age, it has to first manage self. It makes a hard decision midway. In its 40th year, its long and flexible talons become weak and are unable to grab the prey. Its sharp beak becomes bent. Its feathers become heavy and make it difficult to fly. To survive, it has to go through the process of change. It sits on its nest and knocks its beak against the rocks till it plucks out. It waits for the new beak to grow so that it can pull out its talons. After the talons grow, it then plucks out its feathers.

A painful process that ensures it continues to respond to the environment it operates. Thereafter, it lives for another 30 years.

2.5 End of 20th Century/early 21st Century – Environment to Foster Creativity and Innovation

The use of computers in the third industrial revolution quickly expanded to employ Artificial Intelligence (AI). This demands a balance between human consciousness and business opportunity. The aspect of consciousness deals with ethical leadership, building trust and emphasizes on good governance. This is one of the crucial periods in the industrial revolution. We saw the financial crisis in the United States in the early 21st century, which led to the collapse of financial/ banking giants like Lehman Brothers. Building trust was crucial for survival. The financial and housing crisis in the United States propagated the concept of *Prachaar* – the need to create an environment both internal and external for sustainable operation. The aspect of *Prachaar* saw a blend with the second aspect of *Aachaar* which was to do with value-based profit generation. This technological age can be called the 4th industrial revolution (Industry 4.0).

The challenge for the organization was "how to keep people self-motivated" so that they can work with more commitment. Trust deficit among the employees as well as customers was high during the financial crisis in the USA. Committing people to work with a sense of fulfilment and at the same time helping them to overcome the fear of losing a job was the biggest challenge.

But how do we commit a person to work?

Fear of Losing a Job – External Factor

A company was formulating a marketing strategy to launch a product. Time was of the essence in getting the competitive edge over the rival company. The plan was presented and discussed among top management. Everybody appreciated the plan and sought its immediate implementation to maintain the element of surprise over the competitors. However, the Production Head asked for more time to evaluate the changes required in the shop floor during the production stage. Even after weeks, no response was forthcoming from Production Head despite a repeated request from various stakeholders. Precious time was being wasted and fear of competitors getting a hint of new product strategy was looming large. The company's CEO called up Production Head and said, "If this very moment, you do not give your inputs, you are fired." The Production Head said, "The plan can be implemented immediately. Changes, if necessary, can be addressed during the intervening period of product design."

The CEO asked," Why did you waste so much precious time and did not give your go-ahead earlier?" The Production Head replied, "Sir, nobody explained the importance of time, the way you did."

Value Aided Progression gained importance after the financial crisis in the United States in 2008. Organizations realized that the need to create the right environment for positive believing (which is acting on what you believe), with emphasis on social well-being, relationship management, mutual respect, and good association is an essential ingredient to commit a person to work. The same also needs to be communicated to the society to enhance their trust which had been drastically eroded. Organizations now realized the importance of a self-motivated and committed employee. But the question was "*How do you create the right environment if you do not understand the employee's wants and needs?*"

More and more organizations started to focus on developing a Value System intrinsic to the character of the organization. If an employee starts to believe in the Value System of the company and identifies the same with his Values, he is convinced to aim higher and achieve better and bigger. It involves changing the behaviour of people, which originates from their belief system.

Innovation became the keyword not just for technology but even for human survival. Today, organizations are focusing on creating an ambience where people can produce original ideas and foster pioneering work so that they do not lose a motivated employee. It was a shift towards bringing an employee's "heart along with their physical being and mind" to the organization. There has been a tremendous change in the organizational thought process from "the fear of losing a job to the fear of losing a committed employee" – a dramatic change in perspective, indeed.

Would You Lose Such an Employee – Internal Factor

A bunch of tiny frogs arranged a race. The finish point was marked at the top of a very high tower. Many people had gathered around the tower to witness the race and to cheer them. When the race began, nobody believed that any of the tiny frogs would finish the race. Among the cheers, they were loud murmurs that "Finish point is very high" or "They are too small to continue climbing". Many frogs starting collapsing after climbing a few floors. The remaining frogs continued with vigour even though the crowd continued to yell "No one will make it".

One by one all tiny frogs got tired and gave up except the one, who continued to climb higher and higher. Eventually, he reached the top. All other frogs were very curious to know how he managed to do it? When the contestant asked the tiny frog, what was his motivation to succeed, it turned out that he was DEAF. No amount of negative shouting could discourage him. He always considered all the gestures as encouragement from the crowd and continued.

"Great spirits have always encountered violent opposition from mediocre minds."

Albert Einstein

In ancient Indian Gurukul system, the students (shishya) reside at the home of the Guru (Teacher). He was given a holistic education involving every aspect of life. He was given knowledge of scriptures, mathematics, philosophy and language. He also got trained on the use of weapons. The shishya was made conscious of the importance of culture, values, ethics and morality in society and the delivery of justice. The bonding among the shishya creates an environment of brotherhood, humanity and love. The focus was not only to increase their knowledge but also to bring about a sense of discipline, critical thinking and mindfulness to equip them to be able to make correct decisions. Students who emerged as leaders were those who were able to make the correct choices in life and avail and utilize every chance to excel.

More and more companies are focusing on this ancient concept of "Indian Gurukul Age", albeit in a transformational way. Organizations are making an effort to merge knowledge with the organizational value system, morality, ethical behaviour and code of conduct. It is a culture where everyone in the family can imbibe the "Value System" of the company. Innovative perks help employees foster better bonding, team spirit and communication.

There was a time when the product cost was all that mattered. The lowest bidder would get the orders. Today's scenario is however different. Lower cost, better quality and superior after-sales service cannot guarantee you a contract in the current environment. It is imperative to imbibe the cultural ethos of the company to become a vendor. Many companies have even begun considering vendors as partners or associates.

Today, selling is not only left to the sales team. More and more synergy are being created among various department to understand the need and requirement of the client. Who are the decision-makers? What is the client current focus area? Are they image-conscious about community sustainability? Are they more environmentally conscious? Are they willing to pay a premium and help in sustaining the vendors if client focus area is also imbibed by the vendor? All such inputs cannot be decided by salesperson alone. These are few among the many inputs that an organization looks for from its various departments. There is an inherent problem in our education system which is more focused on imparting knowledge specific to the area of specialization. Organizations are now focusing on personality development, creation of moral conscience and ethical behaviour to meet the growing challenges of technological impact and social change. A wrong management decision, which may have heavy financial implications on the company, may be allowed to slide in the name of error of judgement. However, a slack in ethical behaviour is viewed with much strong concern and can lead to more stringent action. It has much wider implications both for the person concerned as well as for the corporate.

Earlier we ideologically believed that hard work alone would help us earn more and would give us all the comforts in life. The money earned through hard work would give us a comfortable life. We would then be happy. However, the focus has now changed to creating an environment in which we are happy to contribute. A happy environment motivates us to put in the extra efforts, which helps us reap better economic benefits. Lack of stressful or conflicting external stimuli enhances our performance. Happiness is now becoming an important and primary criterion. Happiness enhances creativity, innovation and brings originality in our thinking. Creativity in work is the new driving force. It won't be wrong to say that an inspiration stems from innovation, provided by a nourishing environment.

2.6 Building Character – The Emerging Dimension

The Tata group is one of the organizations, which has followed Value Aided Progression (VAP) since its inception. The group was founded by the visionary leaders Late Shri JN Tata. He had dreamt of setting up a steel plant, a hydroelectric network and a university of science. His character is reflected in his commitment to ensuring that his vision fructifies. In 1896, Jamsetji Tata had offered half his fortune worth over three million rupees to the British Government to establish a university of science. He wanted the British government to make an equal contribution and pass enactment to make the university. He did not live to see the light of the day of his dreams. But in his will, he had urged his sons not to touch the benefaction for the university. He urged them to add more to make the university a reality.

> *"Be sure to lay wide streets planted with shady trees, every other of the quick-growing variety. Be sure that there is plenty of space for lawns and gardens. Reserve large areas for football, hockey and parks. Earmark areas for Hindu temples, Mohammedan mosques and Christian churches".*

> *Jamsetji Tata to his son Dorabji Tata in 1902.*

Jamsetji's vision and values reflected his character. Tata Steel introduced the 8-hour work schedule, a worker-friendly policy, chose to give part of their profit to charity and introduced the term Corporate Social Responsibility, much before the nation had even thought about it. Although Jamsetji Tata did not live to see it all realize during his lifetime, the values he nurtured, all his life, has been strongly embedded in the character of the organization – a culture of care and trust for the employees and the society. Many of Tata Steel advertisements also focus on this aspect. "We also Make Steel" was a landmark advertisement of Tata Steel corporate culture. It had become synonymous with the character of the Tata Group.

After the financial crisis of 2008, organizations have demanded more accountability from the senior leaders. The leadership provided by the senior management is a reflection of the character of the organization. We have seen CEOs of big corporate being questioned on probity and integrity.

Wells Fargo, one of the largest bank in the US had to repeatedly apologize for its various misdeeds. Wells Fargo CEO, Mr John Stumpf, was questioned by US Senator Ms Elizabeth Warren on the misconduct. "I am accountable," said Mr Stumpf. But he was asked by Ms Warren, "What have you done to be accountable? Have you resigned as CEO and Chairman of Wells Fargo? Have you returned one nickel of the millions of dollars you were paid when the scam was going on? Have you fired a single senior executive who led community banking division or clients division?" Mr Stumpf replied, "No".

"So", questioned Ms Warren "You have not resigned, not returned any money, and not fired any senior executive. Instead, you have pushed the blame on low-level employees, who do not have money to defend themselves. It is gutless leadership".

True Leadership is all about creating and encouraging ideas in other's minds and inspiring them to take decisions. It is the ability to create more leaders by empowering them rather than by controlling them. Being able to differentiate between Pseudo Leaders and True Leaders is crucial. Pseudo Leaders always look for personal benefit. It can be by way of playing with emotions and sentiments of the people like so many self-styled "Gurus" or "Manipulators", who always devise innovative ways to swindle money.

On the other hand, true leaders or successful leaders have always emphasized on the importance of a value system to drive the inner potential of people or employees. For people to behave themselves in a responsible and committed manner, it is essential to remain motivated. This can be achieved by creating a sense of belongingness to the organization. People just want to ensure their commitment to the organization with the same depth as they feel committed to their respective families.

Summary

- *Business priorities have seen a shift from Cost to Quality to Service. In the last three decades, there is more emphasis on Change management, Creativity and Character building.*

- *Producing goods or offering services at a low cost is important. But lose of customer due to poor quality is the actual cost you incur.*

- *If the business responds successfully to the environment it is operating, then the change process is on the path of accomplishment.*

- *For any change process to be effective, cohesive action on Information & Data (Knowledge), Expertise and Aspiration (IDEA) is essential.*

- *Aspiration needs to create a pull system for Knowledge and Expertise to create the balance.*

- *Creating an environment where innovation and creativity thrives, is critical to be a winner in the future.*

- *Accountability of senior management is vital to create an exclusive character of the organization and to demonstrate true leadership.*

Action Plan

"First and most obvious – bring out the three old warhorses of competition – cost, quality and service – and drive them to new levels, making every person in the organization see them for what they are, a matter of survival."

Jack Welch

- Identify the area where production, quality and cost are being compromised.

"It takes months to find a customer... seconds to lose one."

Vince Lombardi

- Identify the area where service quality is critical. Service would include safety, environment care, hygiene etc.

- List areas where change management is critical.

"The secret of change is to focus all your energy not on fighting the old but on building the new."

Socrates

- List technological challenge faced by the organization in comparison to its competitor.

_____

_____

- Within your domain, ascertain ten areas where organization values are at the difference with what is being done within your domain area. Against each identified area, write down what action has been taken by you to address the situation.

_____

_____

SECTION II – VICHAAR

Chapter 3

A Stepping Stone to Developing Culture and Self-Awareness

The world is becoming a global workplace. The exchange of ideas and thought process takes just a few nanoseconds. In today's environment, every organization needs to anticipate and re-engineer their inbuilt ability, skills and attitude to match the pace of this technological advancement. The organizational philosophy should be able to enhance the mental capacity to improve the thought process of its people to empower them to sustain the pressure, stress and anxiety which they confront each day. Only then can an organization sustain the breakthrough transformation which the industry is going through. This can be achieved by creating more awareness among its people regarding their inherent capabilities and enabling them to manage themselves better.

The success rate of the concept of *Vichaar* in an organization would depend upon the kind of values it has inherited or is attracted to. That will decide the kind of choices an organization will make as well as their willingness to avail every chance in future to improve themselves and make the best out of it.

3.1 Culture – Developing the Business Immune System

Corporate culture is the immune system of a business. It gives the strength and ability to fight back and not get influenced by bad practice and wrong information. Development of wrong corporate culture can create inequality and differences within an organization during the formative years itself. The future principles and conviction of the people in the organization will be affected. Not nurturing ethics, morality, and good governance can lead to the rapid decline of the company. In the recent past, many companies in India have collapsed or are on the brink of closure due to this. Some instances being Gitanjali Gems & Jewellery, Kingfisher Airlines, Nirav Modi and many more. The list can go on and on.

It all boils down to the kind of culture that has been imbibed during the initial and expansion stages of the organization. Onboarding candidates for leadership roles to steer the company should be manoeuvred carefully. Let me illustrate with an example to drive home my point.

The selection committee which shortlisted Mr Vishal Sikka to lead Infosys, in my opinion, had not given enough emphasis on the culture of the organization where he had earlier served. The culture of Infosys was very different and has been very diligently nurtured by its founders. Mr Vishal Sikka was appointed CEO & MD of Infosys in June 2014. He was also Executive Vice Chairman. After three years at the helm, he had to step down in August 2017. Mr Sikka was educationally as well as professionally very competent to head Infosys. Before he joined Infosys, he was the member of the Executive Board and Global Managing Board of SAP AG. He was selected by an international search committee, appointed by Infosys, to lead the organization. Founder CEO & MD of Infosys, Mr Narayana Murthy had taken the initiative to personally introduced him to the company on his appointment and was given the mantle to lead. One tends to ponder, what could have gone so wrong in three years? The founding promoters led by Mr Narayana Murthy had discovered serious governance issues related to the values of the company. If left unchecked, it would have led to consequential implications in the long run and would have negatively impacted the way business had been nurtured and grown in the past.

In 2019, the Mergers and Acquisitions (M&A) between Larsen & Toubro Mindtree also reflected this aspect. The IT industry has always been a people-led organization and every company has its own culture. Mindtree had a very informal culture in comparison to Larsen &Toubro (L&T), a conglomerate, with a top-down management approach, a culture based on command and control. One of the junior employees of Mindtree remarked "*I am not thinking about job security. The only thing that bothers me is whether the work culture which I enjoy in Mindtree, will continue under the new promoter or not.*"

Highlighting another example of M&A is between Gillette with Procter and Gamble (P&G). Gillette had resisted takeovers in the past, one by Revlon in 1986 and again by P&G in 1999. However, when P&G succeeded to take over Gillette in 2005, analyst felt that there would be a challenge integration of the workforce and the cultures of the two organizations. This stemmed particularly because P&G had recently acquired Wella AG, a German hair care firm in 2003 and its integration was still in process. The merger was successful since both the companies had a lot of similarities – a corporate history more than a century old, billion-dollar brands, pioneering consumer product marketing initiative, brand positioning and corporate culture. The product line was complementing each other with P&G's main focus being on women's care and Gillette's on men's care. Both companies also had a healthcare product line. The merger was expected to bring tremendous synergy. In a way, it was also aligned to meet the challenges of online retailing business which was expanding at a very fast pace. *James Kilts, CEO of Gillette & Co remarked: "This marks the realization of a historic next phase of great opportunity for Gillette and P&G. It brings together two companies that are complementary in their strengths, cultures, and vision to create the potential for superior sustainable growth."*

Managing people, talent retention and maintaining cultural identity is very crucial for business progression. Good corporate culture helps in maturing the business process and increasing its life cycle. Business expansion by way of M&A will be on the rise due to technological advancement. A good corporate culture will help in consolidation of business, creating better bargaining power, scaling operation, increased product line, higher productivity and lower cost for a similar scale of operation. The leadership needs to focus on retaining the corporate culture during the expansion stage of the business cycle. It is important for nurturing the next generation for the leadership role. All organization now very fiercely protect and preserve their cultural identity.

For business associates and partners, it is now essential to understand the culture and focus area of the corporate with which they associate, apart from the core business. For many companies, the environment could be the thrust area while for others it could be safety, drinking water, education, health care, sports and so on. If you happen to interact with an organization, which emphasizes on the environment, even if your product or services are costlier than your competitor, you are likely to get the contract because it is more aligned with the corporate culture of the organization. Any organization which focuses on safety will happily pay you extra for following all safety norms. You may even be preferred over other vendors if your safety rating is high. If you wish to sell a product or offer services or register as a vendor in an organization, paying a premium price is not an issue if you are aligned with their culture. For them, the lowest bidder is not the sole criterion.

Good culture is not just the immune system for business sustainability. It is an essential ingredient in every walk of our lives. Whenever we visit a cantonment, we see a visible change in the entire surrounding. The area is very clean, properly marked and people follow rules with a sense of discipline. It is akin to building a culture which reflects your character. Are only a few people responsible to maintain such serenity? Certainly not. It has to be a collective effort, involving everyone – officers, jawans, JCOs, families, children, outsourcing staff, visitors, retinue staff, maids, and every individual who live and use the facility.

Business exists as an individual entity. The psychology and mind mapping of the people who run the business is important in determining the outcome of the business. Nurturing a business culture at the initial stage will determine the kind of value system its employees will imbibe in the future. It is a very important and essential element since the future conduct of business determines this aspect. Maintaining a good organizational culture is imperative for any organization, be it a government, an NGO or even a family. The organizational culture needs to be built on trust, integrity, honesty, heritage, value and tradition. Developing a culture needs sustained efforts. At times, we also need to penalize people for deviating from the cultural ethos.

The management and business operation has to realize that the ownership of the thought process is equally important as the production process itself. Development of organizational culture involves moulding the thoughts of people. But every individual has his thought process. Integrating and aligning it with the organization's thought process is an involved process. The induction training and subsequent interaction must emphasize on this behavioural aspect with a focus on:

- Self Awareness – through the affirmative thought process.

- Building a positive attitude
- Developing a nourishing culture

3.2 Thoughts – Your Starting Action Point

"Doubt yourself and you doubt everything you see. Judge yourself and you see judges everywhere. But if you listen to the sound of your voice, you can rise above doubt and judgment. And you can see forever."

Nancy Kerrigan – A US figure skating champion

In Indian tradition, we light lamps after sunset. This is because we believe that light signifies the end of darkness. It signifies knowledge. A traditional lamp with oil and a wick has a significance. The oil signifies our negative tendencies or ignorance and wick signify our ego. When the lamp (knowledge) is lit, the oil is gradually absorbed and the wick also burns off with it in time. The flame always burns upwards signifying that only knowledge can take us forward. Even though a flame may flicker in winds, but its presence is meant to dispel darkness. One can argue that darkness can also be dispelled by switching on a light bulb. However, such a light bulb only signifies outside illumination. It cannot illuminate you from within. Intramural enlightenment comes from rumination of your mind and the way it's set to think – your thoughts (your Vichaar)

Similarly, our commitment, hard work and conviction will lead us from failure to success. These characteristics dispel the despondency of darkness which surround us when faced with failures and usher us into the light of success.

The negativity of the mind can be controlled. The mind needs to be constantly reminded that there are more positives in life than negatives. If we start monitoring our thoughts, we will realize that we have the ability to allow only positive thoughts to enter our mind.

"The mind is everything. What you think you become."

Buddha

In September 1994, the city of Surat, in the state of Gujarat in Western India, was struck by an outbreak of pneumonic plague. It led to large scale migration, possibly the highest since the independence of India. It was estimated that more than 2,00,000 people fled the city. Surat was then considered as one of the dirtiest and unkept cities in India. At the peak of the epidemic, people were scared to visit their loved ones. The district administration and the residents themselves fought against the epidemic. The moment health and sanitation staff are equipped with adequate protective clothing and necessary precautions are promulgated to handle the crisis, the human mind accepts the same and believes themselves to be immune to the epidemic. It signals that there is a safety zone for all in it. This conditions the mind to accept the outside hostile environment even though most of the preparation takes place with the conditioning of the mind. Within one month, the WHO team declared that the disease was not as widespread as has been reported. They urged the international community to remove travel restrictions imposed on India. Within a decade, under the new municipal corporation team, the city embarked on a cleanliness drive. Since then, Surat has regularly featured within top ten cleanest city in India till 2017. Same was the case of SARS in China or the present case of a novel coronavirus which is considered to have originated from the wet markets of Wuhan, China.

A thought marks the beginning of our feelings. It can embolden us as well as weaken us depending upon the degree of our acceptance. Hence, it is essential to control our thoughts. Although, we would never allow a thief to enter our house, however, we do allow negative thoughts to seep into our minds thereby, depriving us of our peace of mind.

Hence, positive thoughts are the initiation process for a powerful mind which can then be opened for action. The mind is nothing but a flow of thoughts. It is like water flowing through a river. If the water gets dirty, the river is considered impure. Similarly, the purity of thoughts determines the purity of minds. Therefore, understanding the dimensions of thoughts is very important to improve the quality of our lives. Any thought has three basic components – the quantity, its quality, and the direction.

The Quantity of the thoughts deals with the frequency or number of thoughts, which crosses our mind. If the number increases, our mind gets anxious and you are unable to focus. The number of thoughts can be controlled by disciplining the mind. Choose to be the person who is actively, consciously thinking your thoughts. For example, when a student is writing an exam, the focus is always on the question and answer sheet. Nothing disturbs him/her. When a sportsperson participates in a competition, his focus is always on the game. The quantity of the thought can be decreased by the filtration mechanism. We filter and pursue only those thoughts which are relevant. This can only be achieved with an alert mind. Controlling the quantity of thoughts help you to achieve a greater level of peace in your mind. It is the same as we experience while sleeping. The mind just disappears. We have a peaceful sleep when there are no thoughts.

The Quality of thoughts is also determined by the association we keep. If we are in good company, good thoughts will occur. A thief will only think of cheating and stealing. A drug addict will always think of drugs. If we want to change the quality of our thoughts, we need to change the company we keep. Our value system has a great influence in deciding the quality of our thoughts. What is good or bad for an individual is determined by its value system. One person may find eating non-vegetarian food wrong. For another, it may be right. It all stems from the value system one has imbibed. We need to surround ourselves with positive and smart people who can remain positive and challenge our thinking at the same time. Alternatively, we can read, watch or listen to intellectual things to upgrade the level of our thinking. Share them with others so they can upgrade with us. If we leave them behind, we will end up alone.

The direction of flow of thought is determined by the above two considerations –the quantity and the quality. Thoughts always flow in one direction. While writing an exam, a student's thought is always flowing to seek answers. If we are upset about something or angry, everything around us appears distorted. If we are happy, everything looks pleasing.

Let me illustrate the above aspect with an example.

A young man joined a company after finishing his graduation. After spending a few months, one day he walked to the HR head and submitted his resignation. The HR Head enquired about the reason for his resignation. The young man replied, "Most people in his office spends time in gossips. There is hardly any productive work being done here." The HR Head listened to him patiently and said, "I will give you a simple task to perform. If you can do it properly then I shall accept your resignation." The HR Head then gave him a glass full of water and asked him to go round the office without spilling the water. The young man took the glass of water and carefully moved around the office space. On completion of the assigned task, the HR Head asked him, "How many people did you notice gossiping in the office and how many people were engaged in productive work?" The young man replied," I did not notice it since my focus was on the glass of water." The frequency of thoughts, its quality and direction were all focused on the glass of water. The HR Head said, "Young man, had you focused on your work, you would have contributed more efficiently." The young man realized his mistake and took back his resignation.

Hence, it all boils down to, "How we manage our thoughts" The answer lies in self-introspection. We can watch thoughts and emotions to find the source of our sufferings. Introspection is a diagnostic tool for mental ailment. Our mind projects our thinking onto the outside world. We perceive things with this projection and label them as good or bad. If we regularly do self-introspection on our thoughts, it will prevent us from bad influence. And we all know that prevention is better than cure.

3.3   Understanding Self

The first step is self-introspection which leads us to self-awareness. Two qualities essential for self-awareness are:

- Believe in Oneself. If you have low self-esteem, waiting and expecting others to generate confidence in you is pointless. Gaining confidence has to be a journey chalked out by oneself. Others cannot make life's roadmap for you.

- Have a positive attitude.

3.3.1   Believe in Oneself

The first characteristic essential for personal growth is to "*Believe in Oneself*". "*A wise man changes his mind, a fool never will.*" And "*Be the change you want to see around you.*" These famous proverbs go on to emphasize that change is inevitable and to change a situation, you need to believe in the motto, "*We can do it.*" People can only occasionally guide you through difficult times but we have to take our own decision in life. We must be able to steer the wheel of our life and decide which direction to pilot it. Walter Wintle has famously said *"Life's battles don't always go to the stronger and faster man, but sooner or later the man who wins is the man who thinks he can"*

Positive thoughts always enhance our intellectual ability to judge and to discriminate. Two factors instrumental to sharpen our intellect are:

- Be non-judgmental – We are mostly unaware of the factual situational circumstances of another individual. Hence, judgements and opinions formed, devoid of such a vacuum, cannot be just. Perspectives change with our association depending on with whom we want to be associated to.

- Realize that you are unique – Gennen Roth, a writer and teacher of international repute once said, *"There is a vitality, a life force, energy, a quickening that is translated through you into action, and because there is only one of you in all of the time, this expression is unique. And if you block it, it will never exist through any other medium, and be lost. The world will not have it. It is not your business to determine how good it is, nor how valuable, nor how it compares with other expressions. It is your business to keep it yours clearly and directly, to keep the channel open"*.

Therefore, there can only be one original you. Nobody can replace you.

Be Non – Judgmental

Perspective is a mere opinion. It may not be the truth. Based on our perception, we judge a situation and accept the challenges in life – either as tough or as simple. Our positive thoughts enhance our ability to handle them effectively until they start to look easy. We all face some adversities in our life during our growing days. Parents try their best to give equal attention and opportunities to all their children. In low-income groups, there may be situations where unfortunately one child may have to sacrifice for the sake of other siblings due to harsh economic conditions. But the success in life depends upon how we face the adversity. If you put a potato, an egg or coffee beans in boiling water, the outcome is vastly different. A hard potato becomes soft. The egg, which is soft from inside, becomes hard. The coffee mingles with water to give it a unique flavour. The outcome of any adverse situation is decided by what we choose – whether we react or respond to a situation. Whenever we respond, inherently we evaluate the situation. It gives us a choice – to accept or to reject or to stay neutral. When we react, we lose the ability to evaluate a situation. It is always said in the marine world, *"A smooth sea never makes a skilful mariner".*

"Adversity always presents opportunities for introspection".

Dr APJ Abdul Kalam

Our success depends upon how we perceive a situation. All information, which we gather through our sensory organs, is processed in our mind. The mind already has a memory of the past and the experiences of the present. Our perception based on education, interest, experience, past memory and attitude related information, greatly influences our decision-making ability. It leads to selective interpretation. What we perceive ultimately becomes a reality for us. It becomes "One with ourselves." But we can enhance our decision-making ability by learning from other people's experiences. Perception changes with our association. It is important who we associate ourselves within our lives. Hence, good company, is a company of clever and well-informed people who can keep our mind stimulated with positive thoughts while steering us to the path of self-realization and self-betterment.

How You Visualize Is How You Decide

A shoe manufacturing company sent his two salesmen to a new territory to investigate the potential market capability. They reported back saying:

The first salesman, "There is no potential here – nobody wears shoes."

The second salesman, "There is massive potential here – nobody wears shoes."

"When you visualize, then you materialize." Here, we can see how the same situation was perceived differently

by two different salespeople. The second salesman had a positive outlook when he visualized a huge market for the company in the given circumstances, while, the first salesman visualized a dead end and came with negative feedback.

Association with good people helps in forging a good relationship. We use computers daily in our lives. *Even the makers of the keyboard have decided to keep "U" and "I" next to each other.* In the human body, the eyes always blink together, move together, and weep together, even though they are physically separate. A relationship does not mean physical knowing. It is about influencing human minds. The more minds and heart you can touch and influence, there will be an enhanced growth with the outside world which will leave you empowered.

Swami Vivekananda has very beautifully described the meaning of the word "*Association*". He said

"The raindrops from the sky.

If it is caught in the hands, it's pure enough for drinking;

If it falls in the gutter, its value drops so much that it can't be used even for washing your feet;

If it falls on a hot surface, it perishes;

If it falls on a lotus leaf, it shines like a pearl;

And finally, if it falls on oyster, it becomes a pearl.

The drop is the same, but its existence & worth depends on whom it associates".

Taking pride in one's work or other aspects of life be it culture, heritage or values should never be construed as ego. An egotist is not one who thinks too much of himself, but, one who thinks too little of other people. Ego within an organization can destroy team spirit and block growth and hence the road to success. On the road to success, there is always room to share appreciation and gratitude for other's successes. Feeling gratitude for other people raises our vibration while adding cement to the bricks we lay. Finding the best qualities in others allows us to build those qualities within ourselves. When we focus on our personal growth with open hearts and minds, the speed with which we construct dramatically increases, because all the while, we are attracting more energy and like-minded people into our lives to assist us. This is how we pave the way to building strong like-minded relationships.

In Hindu tradition, there is a significance attached to the practice of offering a coconut during religious rituals. Several interpretations have been put up by religious experts to this significance. One of which is that the breaking of coconut is considered as the breaking of our ego (*Ahankara in Sanskrit*) because God expects his devotees to be egoless and pure. The kernel within represents our brain. It is filled with inner juice. This represents the internal tendencies of our brain to be jealous, egoist, selfish human being. Usually, the inner juice is poured out before offering the coconut to God, which means that, we should remove our greed and ego. So, breaking of coconut stands for surrendering to god with utmost selfless devotion and love. Only then we can build a true relationship.

No man is an island. Hence, no business can succeed without fostering a myriad of healthy relationships and association. By developing a strong working alliance with your employees and creating an atmosphere and culture, conducive to developing a strong sense of teamwork, you will be able to increase morale, productivity, and job satisfaction. It will also better enable you to attract and maintain key talent. Thankfully, through fostering relationships, you can bring a human face to your organization – one that customers can relate to and even come to love.

You Are Unique – a Distinctive Individual

Be a Believer to Be an Achiever

"The professor stood before his class of 30 senior molecular biology students, who were about to appear for their final exam. "I have been privileged to be your instructor this semester, and I know how hard you have all worked to prepare for this test. I also know most of you are off to medical school or grad school next fall," he said to them.

"I am well aware of how much pressure you are undergoing to keep your GPAs up, and because I know you are all capable of understanding this material, I am prepared to offer an automatic 'B' to anyone who would prefer not to take the final test."

The relief was audible, as several students jumped up to thank the professor and departed from class. The professor looked at the handful of students who remained and offered again, "Any other takers? This is your last opportunity." One more student decided to go.

Seven students remained. The professor closed the door and took attendance. Then he handed out the final exam test paper. There were two sentences typed on the paper, "Congratulations, you have just received an 'A' grade in this exam. Keep believing in yourself."

Story by Harvey Mackay

"Whatever a human mind can conceive and believe, the mind can achieve".

Have you ever tried dialling your number on the phone? It will say *"All lines in this route are busy. Please dial after some time"*. We often mistake it as a case of incorrect dialling. But truly speaking, it is time for self-reflection. It is time to look within and seek answers. Ultimately, it is only we, who can convert the obstacle into a stepping stone to climb the ladders of success. We need to compete with ourselves to better our performance.

Someone asked a religious guru *"What do you do to seek expert advice"*. The guru replied, *"I talk to myself."* We must first seek answers within. It conditions our mind and prepares us to face the challenges. It is not worthwhile to seek advice from others and not follow it. Talking to yourself mentally prepares us to follow the path of righteousness. It builds up the acceptability within us before we face the situation.

Every individual is unique. It is said that God has created seven people with similar facial features in the world. However, each of these seven individuals is one of a kind. Their life is governed by what they have decided to do. Each individual's presence is a gift to the world in its way. You will never realize what qualities of yours have inspired others and they have moved to higher success in life taking lead from your life. Be your inspiration and benchmark yourself. If you compete with yourself, you will better your records.

Every individual is special in their way. It is for us to realize our true potential. It can dawn on us through association, through observation and more importantly through positive thinking. We get so engrossed in our day to day activities that we never realize our true potential. It is important to believe in ourselves.

You are Unique

A little boy went to his grandpa and asked, "What's the value of life?" The grandpa gave him one stone and said, "Find out the value of this stone, but don't sell it."

The boy took the stone to an orange seller and asked him what its cost would be. The orange seller saw the shiny stone and said, "You can take 12 oranges and give me the stone." The boy apologized and said that the grandpa has asked him not to sell it. He went ahead and found a vegetable seller. "What could be the value of this stone?" he asked the vegetable seller. The seller saw the shiny stone and said, "Take one sack of potatoes and give me the stone." "The boy again apologized and said he can't sell it. This way, the boy went to many vendors and finally reached a precious stone dealer. The precious stone seller immediately recognized that it is an expensive ruby. He said, "even if I sell the whole world and my life, I won't be able to purchase this priceless stone."

Stunned and confused, the boy returned to his grandpa and told him what had happened. "Now tell me, grandpa, what is the value of life?" Grandpa said, "The answers you got from various dealers explain the value of our life.

People value you based on their financial status, their level of knowledge, their belief in you, and their risk-taking ability. So, don't fear. You will surely find someone who will discern your true value. You must always believe in your ability. Learn to first respect yourself and don't sell you cheaply.

Author unknown

3.3.2   Have a Positive Attitude

Most of us go through our formal education. We also pick up various skills during our work. But there is one quality which amplifies excellence in life. This quality is a person's attitude towards work or life and application of common sense.

Attitude is the biggest differentiator in life, be it work or home, family or friends. Attitude is the conditioning of the mind. It shows us the way we accept things either positively or negatively. Attitude is a direct result of our belief. It is the reflection of how you feel about yourself.

History is full of people who have shown the courage to face adversities with a positive attitude and have achieved greater feats in their life.

Louis Braille lost both his eyes due to infection. He was sent to blind school where he was taught by a retired soldier to read with embossed dots. Soon he refined the technique and today his method is bringing joy to millions of blind people.

Nick Vujisik was born without hands and limbs. Doctors had said that he will never be able to walk. Still, he learnt swimming, surfing, sky diving and skating and does everything which even a normal human being cannot do. He even owns two companies and employs many people. He is a living inspiration for many people around the world.

It is we who decide what type of day we are going to have today. We can grumble about all that our parents did not give us when we were growing up or feel grateful that they allowed us to be born. Always give your best, be it in a job or a relationship. We create a situation that allows us to either live in misery or joy. We are the architect of our home called "*life*" and we may not get another chance to rebuild our life. Our life today is the result of choices we made in the past. Our life tomorrow will be the result of the attitude and choices we make today. So, seize every opportunity as it were your last and work at it as if it were your best. Take this awesome real-life example.

When he was born, the parents were advised to kill him because he was blind. He survived. The parents gave him the best education they could afford, however, he faced discrimination at school.

He was not allowed to study science even after obtaining 90% in Class X. He sued the government and won the case. He secured 98% in Class XII. He was denied admit card for the IIT engineering entrance exam. He then decided to apply to a foreign university and got selected at MIT, Carnegie Mellon, Berkeley, & Stanford and went on to become the first international blind student to study at MIT, Boston.

He returned to India in 2012 and started the Bollant Industry where 70% of employees are poor & physically challenged.

In April 2017 he was listed in the Forbes Magazine in under 30 List. His company employs 450 people. Even Ratan Tata, Chairman Tata Group, has invested in his company.

I was made blind by the perception of people.

You don't need eyes, you need vision.

He is Srikanth Bolla

Professional knowledge qualifies us to undertake any work. Knowledge is only information. In today's age of the internet, information is not power. If you seek information, there are plenty available on the internet. Actual knowledge is the information which is yet to be comprehended. Timely and correct use of information makes it potent and powerful. But we need to address the issue of how to use the information. Its apt application turns you into either just a knowledgeable person or a highly competent person. Competence is the skill sets required to apply the acquired knowledge in the right manner. How we use our competence depends upon our Attitude. In today's internet age, system hacking is a common phenomenon. We also have hacker one competition. Hacking into someone else's system is illegal and unethical. But, it depends on how we want to exploit our hacking skills – for the benefit of society by making systems more robust or for our personal gains. It is our competence that helps us stand out among the masses. Competence stems from the aspiration to do work over and above our sphere of influence. The desire or aspiration is the driving force for motivation to be successful. Aspiration is very different from wishful thinking. Aspiration is making your wishful thinking work. The aspiration to excel forms the basis of our attitude towards any work. It is the main driving force – our motivation. It amplifies the will to win, the desire to succeed, the urge to reach your full potential. Attitude is the key that will unlock the door to personal excellence.

Desire to Succeed

A young boy asked Socrates the secret of his success. He took him to a river and when they were neck-deep in water, Socrates took him by surprise and dunked him underwater. When the boy started to turn blue, Socrates raised the boy's head. The first thing boy did was to gasp and take a deep breath. Socrates asked him, "What did he want most when he was underwater." The boy replied, "Air". Socrates replied, "That's the secret of success. When you want success as intensely as you wanted air underwater, you will have it."

The only way you are going to have success is to have lots of failures first. *To be successful, you have to have your heart in your business, and your business in your heart.* We need to build a positive thought process in our mind to improve our commitment, competence and ability to handle a difficult situation. A positive thought helps us in making the right choice in our life. *The only thing that can make us unhappy is our negative thoughts.* Don't limit yourself. Many people limit themselves to what they think they can do. You can go as far as your mind lets you. What you believe, remember, you can achieve. Hence, think big and realize big, as, there is nothing called failure. There are just 1000 ways that didn't work out. That should motivate you to look for the alternative way that would work for you and help you realize your organizational goals. I will share a true story which appeared in Reader Digest and one of my friends shared it with me.

How a Password Changed My Life

A young man deeply depressed after his recent divorce. He couldn't focus on getting anything done in his current mood. One morning while sitting in the office, his computer screen flashed, "Your password has expired." The message reminded him that he shouldn't let himself be a victim of his recent breakup. So, he changed the password, "Forgive@ her." He had to type this password several times every day.

The simple action changed the way he looked at the situation and his ex-wife. That constant reminder of reconciliation led him to accept the way things happened and helped him deal with his depression.

We also need to constantly remind us of the good things we want to achieve in life. It keeps us motivated and excited about achieving it.

Our life is an echo. Everything, just like Karma *(The force produced by a person's actions in one life that influences what happens to them in future lives- Cambridge dictionary)*, comes back in life – the good, the bad, the false, and the true. If you want to be treated with compassion, you must treat others with compassion. If you want to achieve something in life, help others accomplish the same in their life. If you expect proficiency from your juniors, demonstrate competence in your work. If you want to earn money, start donating some today. It is a manifestation of the choice we make in our lives, which ultimately finds expression in our belief, behaviour and actions. It applies in all aspects of our life, be it a relationship, works or play. Hence, the choice you make in your life depends upon your "Attitude".

3.4   Building Nation Culture

Nation culture is built by its people. It is the collective responsibility of the people with political leadership at the helm. In today's political spectrum, we do not trust our political masters. They have nurtured a culture of being corrupt. If an honest politician wants to do anything, that too is viewed with suspicion. But we saw a very positive response from the entire nation when the Prime Minister of India imposed a national lockdown to implement self-isolation within the country on 22 Mar 2020 to fight COVID19 pandemic. The entire nation of 1.3 billion citizens accepted and followed his decision and responded by self-isolating themselves. Everyone stayed at home. Citizens even came out at 5 pm to clap and appreciated the efforts of the people engaged in health service, police, military, security staff and others who are risking their lives for others. It was an unprecedented event witnessed worldwide. Nation-building requires the creation of a positive attitude in the minds of all its citizens to behave responsibly.

Imbibing Positive Attitude

Two brothers were born to the same parent. One grew up to become a successful millionaire businessman and loved his family. The other grew up to become a drunkard and would beat his wife daily. On his father's funeral, both the brothers came. One person asked the drunkard brother, why he is not like his brother. What is the inspiration for his atrocious behaviour? He said "My inspiration is my father. My father was a drunkard. He used to beat my mother all the time. I grew up seeing him doing this all the time. What else should I have become?" The person then asked the other brother what is his inspiration for success in his life. The other brother replied "My inspiration is my father. I grew up seeing him a drunkard, beating my mother all the time and ruining our lives. I decided I will never become like this. I have seen the sufferings and decided that my family will never suffer the same way". Both brothers drew inspiration from the same source. Both had the same observations. However, one conditioned the mind for positive action and others for negative action.

China is focusing to build a culture where people are more socially responsible. Just as we have a credit score rating which determines how we behave in managing our finances, they want to have a social credit system. People will be rewarded or punished based on your social credit score. Just as we are denied a loan, credit card, or other credit facilities based on our credit score rating, people will be denied benefits based on their social credit score. China first announced the "social credit system," in 2014. It is based on the idea to reinforce the culture that "*keeping trust is glorious and breaking trust is disgraceful*," You may be penalized for bad driving, smoking in the non-smoking zone, posting fake news etc. The exact details are not known since it is still under the pilot stage. But the penalties may range from being denied air or train travel, limited internet access, not getting a good job, denying children admission to a good school etc. Slowly people are getting used to it. It will ensure a better cultural system in the entire country. In many countries including India, there is a "No Fly List". If you cannot maintain the decorum of being a civilized person, heckle co-passengers, misbehave with the crew members etc. you can be barred from flying. It could be from a few days to a lifetime ban.

India is now rebuilding its culture and character in consonance with its heritage and tradition. Our culture should bring a sense of pride in us. But we have forgotten the same. We had a great sense of pride when the world recognized yoga as a form of spiritual, mental and physical well-being. Yoga has its origin in our country. Restoration of pride among people can only be done by involving people.

Today, we only complain about it by comparing it with advanced countries where people care for the environment. We have a responsibility to give back to nature and hand back a safe and healthy environment for the next generation. Similarly, a company can make progress only if every generation contributes to its progress and profitability. If every business generation only extracts money for its own benefit, the next generation will be left will nothing and it will eventually be closed. Same is the case with our environment.

In the military, it is imbibed during the training stage itself. If you make a mistake, the entire team gets punished. Slowly, you will find that your friends, colleagues seniors, juniors, nobody allows you to imbibe the wrong culture. Social parties are a common phenomenon in military culture. But, if you cannot hold your drink, you are sure not to get an invitation. In the military, physical and arms training is done by Non-Commissioned Officers (NCOs) or Junior Commissioned Officers (JCOs). They do not shy away from giving punishment if standards are not met.

In Indian culture, it is said: "Khichi Hui Kaan Se Mila Hua Gyan Hamesha Yaad Rahta Hai". (The lesson you learn which is given by pulling your earlobes is remembered lifelong).

In ancient India, a person was considered successful if he has achieved success in the chosen profession. It was not merely gauged by the amount of wealth he/ she possesses. A successful person could be a scholar, a warrior, a painter, a dancer or a person in any profession. Success in today's scenario is always measured by economic success. But to have economic progress, we also need to progress in all aspect of life. We need to build a positive character among the general masses – a character which takes pride in its culture, in its heritage and history, and its people.

The character of the people is reflected in the character of the Nation, which becomes its culture. A few years ago, India was perceived as a dirty place with little importance to hygiene. Swatch Bharat Abhiyan, a program to build a toilet, focuses on making a toilet in every household. It needed a mindset to change. Changing the mindset of a billion people is no small task. It requires tremendous perseverance, effort, planning, advertising, and continued commitment at every level. People need to inculcate the habit of not throwing things in public. They need to encourage people to preserve and respect natural resources and public property. But slowly, we now see people taking pride in their culture. Values and culture are now gaining respect and importance. Yoga is a fine example of this aspect. After COVID 19 pandemic, Ayurveda is gaining traction. Ayurveda is one of the earliest schools of medicine known to mankind. Charaka, the father of medicine, consolidated Ayurveda 2500 years ago. It lost its relevance to Allopathic medicine in the last 200 years. Today Ayurveda is fast regaining its rightful place in our civilization.

Indian people are considered intelligent. Now they are also seen as law-abiding citizens. People are willing to stand up for injustice, against VIP culture, against corruption, against people who promote negativity about our culture and values. There is a sense of rebuilding national pride in everyone's mind. Our past glory needs to be restored with economic prosperity. It can only happen with everyone's involvement. It is no more the responsibility of only the Executive, the Legislature or the Judiciary.

Summary

- *Corporate culture is the immune system of a business. It* is the ability to *fight back and not get influenced by bad practice and wrong information.*

- *The management and business operation has to realize that ownership of the thought process is equally important as the production process itself is*

- *Nurturing an organization culture at the initial stage will determine the values system its employees will imbibe in the future.*

- *The organizational culture needs to be built on trust, integrity, honesty, heritage, value and tradition. Developing a culture needs sustained efforts*

- *Your thoughts decide your actions*

- *Believe in Oneself... You are the best person to steer your life.*

- *Association with positive people will change your outlook.*

- *Building relationship and positive believing can have a maximum affirmative impact.*

- *You are one of a kind. Nobody can replace your inherent talent, belief and faith except you.*

- *Attitude is the biggest differentiator in life*

- *Nation culture is built by its people. The character of the people is reflected in the character of the Nation, which becomes its culture*

Action Plan

- Write three instances when your actions made you feel happy and improved your self-esteem.

_____

_____

- Write the names of three individuals who have impacted your life in a positive way

_____

_____

- Recognize the need to develop and cultivate the culture of the organization.

_____

_____

SECTION III – AACHAAR

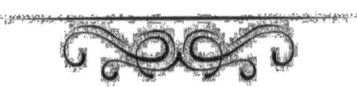

Chapter 4

Self-Management

"Start by doing what is necessary, then what is possible, and suddenly you are doing the impossible".

St. Francis of Assisi

The COVID19 pandemic has made economic prediction very difficult. Unemployment is at its peak. Manufacturing has come to a standstill. Demand is low. Businesses are conserving cash to stay afloat. Every sector is hit and the worst is travel, tourism, and hospitality. However, any adversity also throws up opportunities. India could become a global manufacturing hub if it aligns itself geopolitically and geo-economically post-pandemic situation. Organizations are shifting priorities toward automation. Use of digital technology and artificial intelligence is becoming a new norm even in personal interaction, which otherwise was more restricted to business operation. It has given time for the industry to re-organize and re-build the business around the new hyper-digital world. Online meetings and work from home is the new normal emerging. Although it has helped the organization to curtail its costs in terms of requirement of the real estate office space, the new norm is putting undue stress on individuals. Home privacy is being compromised. The problems of coping with the IT revolution is compounded by the challenges faced by people due to COVID 19. Few questions that frequently crop up are:

- *What will human beings have to do for peaceful sustainability?*

- *Will it create stress in their professional and personal life?*

- *How to succeed in such an emerging situation?*

In future, any conceivable technology, which cannot operate through smartphones is doomed to fail. More and more industries are likely to disappear. There is uncertainty regarding the skills required for and its availability within industries. This brings tremendous pressure on leadership and management.

Many organizations, which have focused more on managing the external environment to suit the internal organization conditions, have failed. Managing external environment in today's scenario is extremely difficult. Organization need to self-equip itself with mechanisms which will lubricate the development and enchantment of business. In my view, this mechanism is through *Aachaar.*

Aachaar deals with two major aspects to translate the organizational philosophy into value-based actions.

- Self –Management skills
- Managing business economics.

Self-management aides to resist stress which emanates from your thinking process. If you can control your thoughts, then you can control your actions. This is the first step to value-based behaviour. Managing self is the key to success in managing change which is the source of all stress. To be successful in today's environment, we need to first understand and manage ourselves. Organizations are constantly working to improve social and work environment to counter the pressures related to physical work and employee's mental ability.

Ultimately, it is the people who lead or enunciate the process of change. Their inability to handle change will increase their stress level. *Organizational values need to be aligned to human values to overcome any internal conflict within people.* Self-managing skills are most important to handle this change process.

4.1 Ability to Perform Versus Ability to Deliver

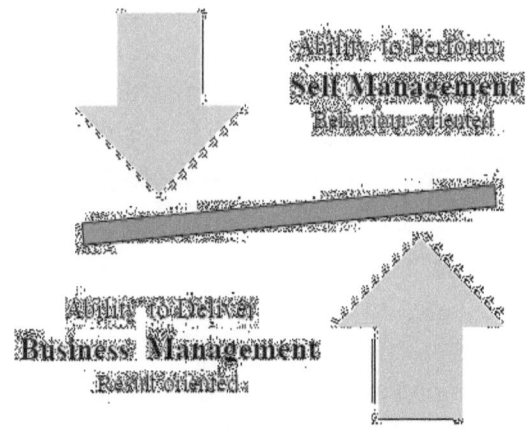

Self-Management is the belief that one can deliver. It is the first step towards the "Ability to Perform". We select people for a particular role based on their educational qualifications, experience, their delivery capability in areas where they have already worked etc. A person also believes that their past achievements qualify them for the higher responsibilities, hence he can be termed as a "Believer". But, situation, culture, ethos and values change from organization to organization. People who cannot adapt to these situations, buckle under pressure and are unable to deliver.

Let us view this with an example which all of us have experienced in India. In the recent past, on 08 November, 2016, the Government of India announced demonetization which meant all INR 500 and INR 1000 currencies would no longer be valid. This sudden decision and implementation created a cash crunch in the country, which in turn affected all business sectors.

Such a situation demands your ability to adapt to change instantly and innovate ways to emerge from the crisis. Handling anxiety in such unforeseen climate is critical to be able to furnish positive outcomes. Self-management is critical to effect delivery on the ground.

It could be that a person may meet all the required criteria essential to qualify for the new role. But they may still be unsuccessful. The understanding of the new role dynamics helps you in the actual delivery in your new role. The new role dynamics may be related to the working environment, culture & ethics of the new organization, attitude of the team members, interdepartmental relationship, understanding people's psychology and their behaviour etc.

To manage self, one needs to understand self. To understand self, one needs to explore self – do a self SWOT analysis (Strength Weakness Opportunity & Threat). Just like Arjuna, one needs to discover the spiritual path to get clarity in thoughts and action. Only then they can move to become an Achiever. Achievement is a result-oriented criterion. It is your "Ability to Deliver". *Achievement signifies result*. It is a long-term criterion. Believing is far different from achieving. It is a move from "*Proficiency*" to "*Efficiency*".

Ability to deliver requires understanding and evaluation of several issues like business economics, the anticipation of the changing environment, understanding of cultural fit of the organization as well as skills like team building, communication, goal-setting, coordination, leadership etc. A person with a very high delivery ability is an "*Achiever*". One needs to bridge the gap from being a *"Believer"* to becoming an *"Achiever"*.

Delivery on Ground Matters – Not Position

A priest dies and goes to heaven. At the gate of heaven, right ahead of him was Muthu, a bus driver. Muthu was very rash and negligent while driving. People boarding his bus always used to pray for their safety and would thank the Almighty on safely disembarking at their destination. The priest, who delivered his daily sermon at a local church was given a cotton robe while Muthu was handed over the silken robe. When the priest protested, Lord said, "My dear when you preached, people slept.

But when Muthu drove, people prayed. It is not your position or performance but what you delivered on the ground that matters".

Let's review in the context of politics and military to see, how self-management skills can improve our decision-making ability and our ability to deliver. The current political environment in India and many other countries need management of coalition partners to ensure the proper functioning of the government and implementation of the policies. For more than two decades in India, the single-party rule has been virtually non-existent. At times, minority stakeholders have more say in the decision-making process because the stability of the government hinges on their support. The leadership should understand and demonstrate mutual respect for other's needs, aspirations and ideology. *To manage others, one needs to demonstrate a very high level of emotional control. In such cases, critical reasoning does not always give the desired results.*

There is very little a military leader can do to manage the external threat environment in a battlefield because of lack of information and uncertainty of the military operation. In a battle scenario, the company leader has to make quick decisions based on available information, contingency planning and trust of his team members. His decision may decide the course of a war and may even risk the lives of the men he commands. He uses his gut feeling, intuition, instinct and trust in his subordinates, to make the right decision. His decision is largely guided by his self-management skills. A soldier's emotion can drive passion among his teammates and at the same time, it can also destroy the mission if mishandled.

A soldier focuses more on managing internal resources which prepares them to meet the uncertainty. The soldier is prepared to manage self, which gives them the ability to manage the stress induced by external conditions. It is this ability of military leadership which brings victory at war, no matter what the strength of the opponent is. *"How are they able to decide about the life of people?" "How will they face the families of their colleagues if their decision goes wrong leading to loss of life?" "How will they answer their countrymen if their decision has major political outfall?"* "How *are they able to take such decisions and still live peacefully, happily, face the families whose members lost their life due to their decision?" "Does it not affect their personal life?" and "How come, the aggrieved families remain friends with them?"* The answer lies in Value-Based Leadership and Self-Management skills. That is the secret of a soldier's success to human happiness.

Today, the conventional military techniques, to handle change, have found their way into the corporate culture. If we want to exploit a person's inherent strength then we need to focus on our organization's value system. Organizations are now focusing on harnessing the inner strength of the employees based on the organization value system. An organization's value system gives a person strength to take calculated risks to stay ahead of their competitors. It makes him think differently. The internal organization culture needs to be strengthened to meet the challenges of the external environment. Sustainability of organization cultural ethos has always withstood the test of time if it is nurtured with diligence.

4.2 Sun of Apprehension Vs Sun of Control

The sun is the source of energy for life on earth. It is the biggest star in our solar system. The outward pressure of the gas, due to the heat it generates in its core, is balanced by the internal pull of the gravity. This keeps the sun in equilibrium. Our life is also governed similarly. If we want to maintain the equilibrium in life, we need to balance the external and internal forces.

Our present is greatly influenced by the memories of the past and dreams of the future. It is said that *"Good judgment comes from a bad experience."* Most of the decisions we take in our present-day life come from memories and impression of good or bad judgment, our knowledge and our experience. It forms the basis to overcome current day apprehensions.

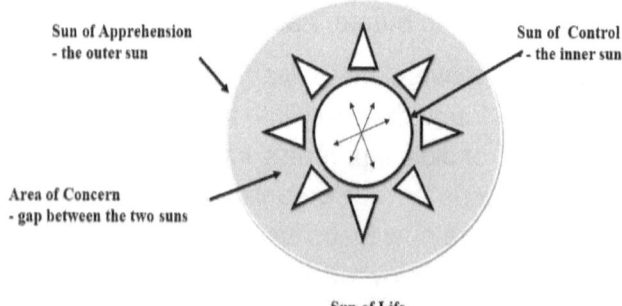

Sun of Apprehension and Control is inspired from Book "Self Managing Leadership published by Brahma Kumaris, page 71

The outer sun is the Sun of Apprehension whereas the inner sun is the Sun of Control. If we can control the gap between the two suns, we can maintain equilibrium in our life.

Self-management is all about expanding your Sun of Control. Apprehensions can arise from many situations, most of which are not in our control. The ability to control is well within our domain. *The gap between these two suns is our concern area.* As the gap increases, our ability to control the apprehension decreases. It leads to undue stress on us. Our decision-making ability reduces. We are prone to make more mistakes which ultimately increases our level of unhappiness.

If the gap between these two Sun decreases, we can control our anxiety better. That way, we can handle uncertainties in life in an improved manner, even when we do not have control over it. We stay healthy which promotes our well-being and guarantees quick setback recoveries.

Sun of Apprehension	Sun of Control
Government Policies	*Values*
Economic Recession	*Belief*
Global competition	*Integrity*
Environmental condition	*Moral Courage*
Socio-political situation	*Character*
Technological Obsolescence	*Trust*

Sun of Apprehensions

External environment uncertainties will always expand the Sun of Apprehension. Following are few of the external environmental stimuli under the Sun of Apprehension on which we have little or no control.

Government Policies

Government lays down policies and frames rules and regulations that guide the economic policies for conducting business. Monetary and Taxation policy can increase or decrease the cost of doing business. Interest rates and taxation not only affects business operation but also spending by the public. Providing subsidy and tax holiday to environmentally friendly technology will impact existing business which is not using the same. Make in India focus on government forced global companies to rethink their strategy.

One of the worst economic recessions which the world has experienced in recent times is the financial crisis of 2008. This apart from the current financial crisis due to COVID19 pandemic, the economic impact for which is yet to be evaluated. Despite all regulatory measures in place, it took more than two years to overcome the financial crisis of 2008. Millions lost their jobs. Fiscal austerity, liquidity crunch, high inflation, falling GDP, higher oil prices, etc. can all affect production and consumption. On the contrary, if the above issues are brought under control or are positive, companies can hire more people, pay higher salaries, and spend more on goods and services.

Global Competition

Today competition is faced by companies from every corner of the world. Japanese cars are manufactured in India and sold the world over. Same is the case with a lot of electronics, steel, toys and a host of other commodities which are produced in China and are available the world over at much lower cost. The World Trade Organization (WTO) deals with international trade policies. Government formulates its international trade policy to safeguard the interest of its citizens and companies. OECD (Organization for Economic Cooperation and Development), IMF (International Monetary Fund) and similar organizations at global and regional levels like NAFTA (North American Free trade Agreement), CAFTA (Central American Free Trade Agreement) have a great impact on the size of the market and extent of the investment to be made, both by domestic as well as foreign companies.

Environmental Conditions

Environmental conditions are related to cultural, political, social, demographic as well as technological conditions, which affects business. Company strategy needs to evaluate all these conditions. The business has an impact on the environment we live in. The environment also has a similar impact on business operations. With increased emphasis on controlling pollution control, promoting

---

1 For example, fossil fuel versus renewable energy. Tax imposition from retrospective dates will impact profitability. The government's focus on a specific area like education, healthcare can boost business in these fields and so on. Fixing minimum wage, employment to a disabled person, minimum women representation in company board, preference to women, health and hygiene maintenance, safety standards, emission norms, employment laws etc., are few examples

greenhouse, correct method of waste segregation and disposal, environment-friendly recycling techniques etc. the business strategy needs to be devised accordingly.

Socio-Political Stability

Socio-Political stability is essential for a conducive business environment. We have seen these in Srilanka, Afghanistan, Syria and so many other countries. Government stability builds confidence in the minds of the corporate for taking timely policy decisions. Companies operating in multiple markets must be sensitive to local cultures and traditions. Social issues can create big impact since local cultures and traditions get recognized at the political level also. Diwali celebration at the White House has a positive influence on American people and products in Indian markets. Indian home-grown FMCG brand, Patanjali, encashed on this very psyche of the Indian customer. It created a business empire by building trust among people and branding its products to evoke swadeshi (made within the country using indigenous ingredients) appeal among the masses. The focus on Ayurveda and organic products equally appealed to the health-conscious higher income group, young generation as well as lower strata of the society. It had an instant connect with the cultural heritage and Indian society pedigree.

Technological Obsolescence

A large number of fortune 500 companies that existed in early 1950 are no longer in the list. Many have closed down business operations and a few have been merged. Digital transformation and technology are the new engines of growth. The company needs to focus more on innovation for survivability. Blockbuster was a home video rental giant. It had operations worldwide and employed more than 70000 people. In 2000, Netflix approached Blockbuster to sell their firm for a sum of USD 50 million. Blockbuster declined considering that it is a small niche business. Today Netflix has more than 100 million subscriber base and revenue above USD 80 billion. Blockbuster filed for bankruptcy in 2010. Compaq was the market leader in personal computers in the 1980s. It could not sustain the price war against Dell and was ultimately acquired by HP. Nokia was the market leader in mobile phones in the late 1900s and early 2000. With internet penetration, they failed to recognize the importance of data as the future of communication. Apple launched the iPhone and became the market leader. Xerox failed to capitalize on technology twice. They were the first to invent the PC. They failed to take the lead on digital invention, thinking it is too expensive. Eventually, they lost on both the counts, Personal Computers as well as photocopy to the digital revolution.

Sun of Control

The human mind is the most powerful supercomputer which helps you to easily adapt to changing situation. The power of the subconscious mind should never be underestimated. It has the power to heel, to motivate, to detach, to influence and to change your life. A conducive environment always helps in enhancing this power by removing the internal conflicts within a person, which is the starting point to counter the pressures of the external environment. It expands your Sun of Control and bridges the gap between the two suns. Let's review some of the parameters that influence the Sun of Control. These are stimuli which are under our control.

Value System

Values system is often characterized by individual virtues or vices which we imbibe. It has a major influence on our behaviour, thinking, attitude, and actions, which determines our ability to deal with situations.

The famous management guru, Peter Drucker has said, "Culture *eats strategy every day for breakfast*". We have seen this in the recent times even with the big corporate house like Tata group and Infosys wherein imposing a different strategic thinking, compromising the cultural values of the organization, had a severe backlash leading to the removal of the top management.

Companies have started to look beyond profits. They want their cultural identity to be meticulously maintained, nurtured and its values need to percolate to the bottom of the pyramid in the organization. Values need to be inculcated during the initial recruitment and training stage itself for a strong foundation.

One of the finest examples of the recruitment process is of the Indian Armed Forces. We have little knowledge about the psychological behaviour of people during the hiring stage. In India, recruitment for the Armed Forces officers is done by a three-stage selection process. First, a candidate has to qualify for a written exam to prove his academic knowledge.

Second, the qualified candidates have to appear for Service Selection Board (SSB). SSB evaluates every candidate on three parameters namely, Psychological Test, Group Activity which includes physical fitness and Personal Interview. It is spread over 05-06 days. During this period, candidates are assigned various tasks, sometimes as a team leader and sometimes as a team member. Situations are thrown with some constraints. Their cognitive ability to find solutions, as team leaders and as members, is evaluated. There are separate evaluators to assess their psychology, group behaviour, physical fitness and personal conduct. A candidate has to independently qualify in each category to get selected. The interview call for SSB is based on the written test or academic results. But selection by SSB is never done on academic excellence. During these 05-06 days of SSB interview, the candidates have to stay inside the cantonment. Their behaviour is studied over this period. Each selector of SSB makes his/ her independent assessment before recruiting any candidate. They focus is never only on academic excellence. And finally, the qualified candidate has to pass the medical board.

Many corporates have started following this model. Case studies are given to candidates. Many offer internships during which they get the opportunity to evaluate a candidate not just for their academic credentials but for a host of other personality development skills like team building, coordination, communication etc. The Armed Force of any country is still regarded as one of the finest services. It is the last bastion to maintain peace, harmony and generate goodwill among masses when regular government machinery fails to deliver. It is one of the most effective government organizations and its officers are held in much higher esteem by the general public in contrast to other services. Why? The reason lies in the selection process and subsequent training. The organization knows that people with technical skills can be trained to suit the organization's requirement.

On 26th Nov 2008, a group of terrorists attacked the iconic then 103-year-old Taj Mahal & palace Hotel in Mumbai. The hotel had around 600 staff on duty and around 1700 guests. The first reaction in any such situation would be to leave the hotel for safety. But surprisingly, during the attack, none of the staff left the hotel even though they were fully aware of all the entry and exit routes. The General Manager of the hotel in an interview said, "I come from Army background. At the time of joining the hotel, my father said, consider yourself to be the captain of the ship. You must be the last to leave the ship. Do not abandon it." The General Manager lost his wife and two young kids during the attack. That day 1600 guests were escorted to safety. Only 34 people lost their lives and half of them were hotel staff. Even the Chefs and kitchen staff took the bullet to ensure the safety of the guests.

Inspired from Ted talk by Rohit Deshpande,*
Faculty Harvard Business School

What motivated them to act in such a manner? Is it the human resource policy or corporate culture, industry requirement or Indian culture where guests are treated as God "Atithi Devo Bhava"? It is more to do with recruitment policy and subsequent training. The front-line staff of Taj Mahal Hotels are recruited from small towns where traditional culture is still given greater importance. During recruitment, they took feedback from the school teachers to understand the employee attitude, cultural inclination and importance to the value system. The respect they demonstrated towards elders, parents, teachers and others. Academic grades are not the criteria for their selection. Their focal point during training was guest and not organization. They are trained to become ambassadors of the guest and not the hotel. Their rewards are not monetary but more focused on recognition. Their reaction during the terrorist attack amazed and stumped many psychologists.

Don't we see a similarity of training and culture with armed forces and its recruitment strategy?

Belief System

Belief stems from hope and faith. It is one of the biggest driving forces or motivators for any human being. It can be likened to the belief a patient has in their doctors, hoping to get a cure for all their illnesses, even though at times, the disease may be incurable. Several times doctors say, "*It is only the prayers or a miracle which can save the person.*" It was this belief system, ingrained in the soldiers of the Indian Army that eventually made them capture icy hilltops in Kashmir from Pakistani occupation despite adverse conditions during the Kargil war.

1883, John Roebling, an engineer, dreamt of building a spectacular bridge across the east river to connect New York with Long Island. His idea was rejected by many experts who found it impractical and dangerous. Subsequently, he could convince his son John Washington and they began work on their dream project. But a few months later, in an accident, John lost his life and his son Washington was paralyzed. Everyone had negative thinking about the project and wanted to scrap it since only Washington was aware of it in totality. Washington was not discouraged. He developed a communication technique with his wife by just moving his finger. His wife continued to communicate his message to his team. 13 years later, the bridge got completed. This is the Brooklyn Bridge in New York.

The story of the Brooklyn Bridge drives home one strong point in our mind. Impossible dreams can be realized by a strong belief system which drives your determination to succeed. It helps you to remain focus on your mission despite failures. **It has the power of driving you to a hopeless end or a conviction of endless hope**.

Just like an elephant whose mind is conditioned to believe that they cannot break the rope to which they are tied at a tender age, many of us limit our potential with the conditioning of our mind from the past. We do not attempt to change it simply because we have failed once. It is important to remember

"We may fail in our attempt but we must never fail to attempt. Falling should never be construed as failing. We fail only when we refuse to get up"

Moral Courage

Moral courage teaches you ways to handle emotions, and uncertainties of life. It is the ability to be accountable and own up mistakes. It is the willingness to face pain, disapprovals without compromising the values and ethical principles. Moral courage helps you to face disappointments in life with dignity. It builds a sense of honour and pride in your achievements. Moral courage is always linked with integrity and the ability to stand strong with your conviction, even when odds may not be in your favour. Holding ground for what you believe is important. But, if you do not act accordingly, then it cannot be construed as moral courage. Standing ground coupled with supportive action defines integrity.

People who have shown moral courage stand out as leaders. In a combat scenario, moral courage and integrity define the boundaries within which the team has to operate. It is a very important virtue which allows any individual to act according to his own as well as the organizational values irrespective of the situational challenges. It builds confidence among team members.

A very famous incident in the annals of recent history is the response of the Israeli government to handle a terrorist attack. Israel gave go-ahead for Operation Thunderbolt fully knowing that failure would lead to the mass killing of its people – the Jews, by the terrorists. It required great moral courage to take such a decision and be prepared to face the consequences in the event of the decision going wrong. A group of terrorists had hijacked an Air France flight carrying 238 passengers and took it to Entebbe in Uganda on 27 June, 1976. Their demand was a USD 5 million ransom and release of 53 known pro Palestine militants, held around the world by 2 pm on 01 July, 1976. They even separated other passengers from Jews and progressively released 132 non-Israeli passengers. The deadline was extended to 04 July, 1976. A day earlier, the Israeli government approved Operation Thunderbolt. It was a bold decision. It was a moral decision considering the government responsibility to take care of its citizens. Negotiations with terrorists could have opened the possibility of risking citizen's life in future. It was also against the stated government policy of non-negotiation with a terrorist. It was a risky operation considering that it had to be carried out nearly 4000 miles away in enemy territory. It was carried out brilliantly and all passengers were rescued. 102 hostages could be rescued. Three got tragically killed in the crossfire and one was brutally murdered by the troops of Idi Amin, the President of Uganda. 04 July is celebrated as America's Independence Day. But Jewish celebrate this day for the most courageous, miraculous and breath-taking operation in the history of hostage release. Many Hollywood movies have been made on this and it is one of the proudest moments for Israel.

'Courage is not the absence of fear but the resistance of fear, the mastery of fear.'

Mark Twain

A Soldier's Father

Mr *Lachhman Singh Rathore, a simple man in his eighties, was informed about the martyrdom of his son, Flying Officer Vikram Singh. On reaching the airbase, he requested the liaison officer to allow him to meet Vikram's friend, see his room and if possible, visit his workplace. He only needs to be informed of the rituals to be followed for the funeral so that he can abide by the decorum.*

When he left the next day, the liaison officer remarked to his boss, "A brave man he is. Spoke to me like a General when he told me exactly what he expected from us during his stay here. I have never seen a more composed man on such an occasion. I admire him." "Yes, Mr Lachhman Singh Rathore is a warrior in his way. He sired three sons and has laid to rest all three of them. His first son Captain Ghanshyam Singh of the Gurkha Rifles was killed in Ladakh in 1962 War. His second son, Major Bir Singh, died along the Ichogil Canal in 1965 in an ambush. His youngest, Vikram Singh, who dared to join the Air Force, is also gone now. He contributed more to our country's defence than all of us combined. "Yes, he is indeed a brave Indian. He is more Indian than anyone else – His sacrifice can never be repaid by the Country!! He is almost a Martyr himself!!

Inspired from a story by WgCdr Venki Iyer

Integrity

Integrity is much more than just being honest. In simple words, it is moral courage in action. It is the ability to take a position even at the expense of losing the affection of near and dear ones. It is integral to building your self-esteem as well as admiration for others. It is like the carbon of your character, which when polished and properly cut, can be shaped into a diamond. It is the foundation, on which your life principles are built. It is your basic virtue which makes you feel proud and not regrets for your decisions. It seeks sacrifice of comfort, possession, friendship etc. to uphold these life principles. Integrity builds trust. It is always measured by others by your "Conduct" and not by your "Position". It is the core of our value system. It gives you the strength to have moral courage. It is a virtue which should not change within the domain of time, space and context. It is the most important ingredient to build character and trust.

---

[2] The importance to maintain personal information integrity can be viewed from the fact that C- suite executive of biggest technology companies like Facebook, Google, Twitter, WhatApps etc. are appearing before Legislative committees to restore users faith and trust in their organizations.

In the current changing environment, social media has invaded our privacy. Many of our personal information is available online. We trust the organization which collects this information, some of who sell these data for advertisement, to gather customers and even for political campaigns. In the world of digital transformation, how secure is our life when we share such information with the unknown organization? Hence, integrity within such organizations must become a cultural custom. Even within organizations, the factor of integrity is critical in building trust at a time when companies operate globally[2].

Story One

Easy Eddie was the lawyer of Al Capone, the underworld don who virtually ruled Chicago. Easy Eddie was rewarded with all the luxuries of life for keeping Al Capone out of prison. But despite his association with not so good people, Easy Eddie always wished to teach his son how to live life with integrity, which he lacked. He realized his mistake and confessed to law enforcement agencies about his involvement and testified against Al Capone. He had to pay with his life for this action. But he had the satisfaction that he could set a personal example for his son to live a life with integrity.

Story Two

Lieutenant Butch O'Hare, a fighter pilot, was one of the heroes of World War II. He single-handedly attacked the Japanese air squadron while returning to the American fleet. His action took the Japanese by surprise. Later, when his ammunition ran out, he crashed his plane with the enemy plane sending them in a downward spiral. His act saved the American fleet from the impending danger of the Japanese attack. He had destroyed five enemy aircraft and managed to land back on his aircraft carrier. He was recognized as the first Naval Aviator to win the Congressional Medal of Honour.

Today, the O'Hare Airport in Chicago is named after his bravery.

So, what do these two stories have in common?

Butch O'Hare was none other than "Easy Eddie's" son.

Character

Character is the total of many qualities which are intrinsic to our value system. It has the power to improve our sense of judgment, compassion, moral courage and ethical behaviour. Most organizations have started to display their core values on their website and publications. It essentially reflects the character of the organization which, epitomizes the intrinsic values expected to be imbibed by every employee of the organization. It reflects the culture of the organization – the collective behaviour expected of its employees.

Character is a summation, a bundle or an assortment of qualities like integrity, the honesty of purpose, faith, and trust which forms the foundation of your belief system. It is your conviction with which you do any job.

Building a strong character is the primary structure on which an organization thrives. It is, however different from the reputation of the organization. The character of the organization can rebuild the tarnished reputation of an organization

Once a lady took two of her kids to a movie. She asked the booking clerk, "How much does the ticket cost?" The booking clerk said, "Rs 100 for you. Kids below five years are allowed free."

The lady replied, "Here is two hundred. One for myself and one for my kid. One of my kid is six years old and the other is four." The booking clerk replied, "You could have easily saved Rs.100. Nobody would have known whether your child is six or five years old."

The lady replied, "I know. And I don't want to teach my kids to lie"

The building of a strong character is one of the biggest outcomes of managing yourself positively. The character of a person determines his behaviour during trying times. Character is the basic nature of a person. Even though, an individual's personality can be faked to suit the situation but not the character. That is because, personality is a perception whereas, and character is imminent.

In recent times in India, the singular mission of building toilets in every household in India reflects the will and character of the nation and the commitment of the government towards hygiene and women's safety. Today, there is a change in the mindset of the people of India. The country is made of its people. It is the will of its people which determines its value system and reflects its character.

Trust

Every individual team member is required to perform his duty with diligence and commitment. Trust in the team member's ability is the essential ingredient in building the team spirit. Do not doubt others capability. In the long term, it will undermine your potential to perform and deliver. The armed forces, in particular, face this situation very often. The soldier at the front always has the risk of facing the bullet. The soldier leading the platoon trusts his teammates for a cover-up or counter-attack if the situation demands. The soldiers following the platoon leader trust him for his sense of judgment and quick decision. Trust comes from the character of a person. Unless an environment of trust is created, we can't expect a person to go beyond his call of duty – the extra mile.

Hold My Hand

A little girl was crossing the river bridge along with her father. The father was concerned that she may slip and asked his daughter, "Sweetheart, please hold my hand so that you do not fall into the river."

The little girl replied, "No, Daddy. You hold my hand."

The father was puzzled. He asked, "What›s the Difference?"

The girl replied, "There is a world of difference. If I hold your hand and slip, chances are there that I may let go of your hand. But if you hold my hand and I slip, no matter what happens, *I am sure you will never let go my hand."*

We have all lifted a child and swung them in air. The child always smiles because the child trusts that you will catch him/her. It requires a continuous and conscious effort over the years to build trust. However, it takes only a second to break it. The cost to repair the trust may take a lifetime. Trust is something you earn or gain over some time. You may respect a person for various reasons however, trust has to be earned. Trust can never be given just like respect.

Trust is also different from loyalty. Loyalty needs to be demonstrated. In armed forces, these words have great importance. You are loyal to the country and your fellow men and are willing to face bullet and lay your life in the line of duty. In return, you trust your fellow men not to leave you even when injured and your country to take care of your family in the event of the ultimate sacrifice. Loyalty is demonstrating your faith in someone else no matter what. Trust is a belief in someone no matter what. All the three aspects -trust, respect and loyalty- are inter-related. It is the duty of the leader that none of them is betrayed or else he will lose all three.

Many employees who sacrificed their lives saving the guests at Taj Mahal & Palace Hotel during the terrorist attack had this trust and belief in the Tata group's Integrity. Possibly, they would not have behaved similarly had they been working in another organization even though the hospitality industry lays immense importance to guest management and treat all their guests with very high esteem. It takes years of commitment, dedication and honesty of purpose to create such a value system in which an ordinary people can have tremendous faith and belief. Tata group has earned that trust of their employees and the outcome was that the employees even took a bullet to save the honour, reputation and values of the organization. It takes years to build such trust.

4.3   Maintain Equilibrium

If we have greater influence over the Sun of Control, it gives a positive response. We don't react negatively to situations. It enhances determination, commitment, perseverance and ability to handle the situation with much more calmness and openness. It maintains our stability and poise to make better decisions. A greater influence on Sun of Control also fosters team spirit, better coordination and pooling of resources to handle the situation in a more comprehensive and coordinated way.

Alternatively, if we are unable to sustain the pressure exerted by the Sun of Apprehension, it builds negativity within us. Our concern area increases which start affecting our personal and professional lives.

Organizations exist because of people. Just as the quality of seed decides the quality of the plant, the self-management control parameters are the foundation of people behaviour. These parameters decide the responsiveness to any situation.

The farmers know the correct climatic conditions, water requirements, type and quantity of fertilizer to be used to grow flora. But if the quality of seed is inferior, the result will be stunted growth. Same is the case with people.

The Story of Watermelons

"I am from the village of Parra in Goa; hence we are called Parrikars. My village is famous for its watermelons. When I was a child, the farmers would organize a watermelon eating contest at the end of the harvest season in May. All the kids would be invited to eat as many watermelons as they wanted. Years later, I went to IIT Mumbai to study engineering. I went back to my village after 6.5 years. I went to the market looking for watermelons. They were all gone. The ones that were there available, were so small. I went to see the farmer

who hosted the watermelon eating contest. His son had taken over. He would host the contest but there was a difference. When the older farmer gave us watermelons to eat he would ask us to spit out the seeds into a bowl. We were told not to bite into the seeds. He was collecting the seeds for his next crop. We were unpaid child labourers. He kept his best watermelons for the contest and he got the best seeds which would yield even bigger watermelons the next year. His son, when he took over, realized that the larger watermelons would fetch more money in the market so he sold the larger ones and kept the smaller ones for the contest. The next year, the watermelons were smaller, the year later even small. In watermelons, the generation is one year. In seven years, Parra's best watermelons were finished.

In humans, generations change after 25 years. It will take us 200 years to figure out what we were doing wrong while educating our children."

By Late Manohar Parrikar,
The ex Defence Minister of India

When India got independence, there was hardly an industrial base. India then and even now is largely an agricultural-based society. Since time immemorial, Indian farmers have produced goods using organic means. Slowly, it changed to chemical-based fertilizer, to hybrid produce and even artificially grown seeds. In the next 60 years, people have forgotten how to use and produce goods organically. The revival process has just started with more and more people realizing the importance of organic food. What was once the only way known to the people of India is now the expensive way reserved only for the health-conscious higher income group, same is the case with Indian history and its rich culture. The textbooks are more focused to elaborate on how external aggressor invaded India, be it Mughals, Afghans, British, or Portuguese. There is little emphasis on the rulers who fought to preserve the integrity, culture and values of our country. Their contribution has little acknowledgement in the Indian heritage. In the last 60 years, three generations have grown with little knowledge about this great Indian civilization. This is because it is never taught in schools. Developed countries have started to recognize the importance of values and contribution of Indian cultural heritage in founding a strong societal base. If we do not act now, it will be too late to rectify. We will lose our cultural identity and contribution of this great civilization to the world.

The foundation of values system, ethics, morality, moral courage and integrity determines the quality of people. They may use or misuse their technical competence based on this foundation. It is also same as families or any social structure. The response of the people depends upon what they have imbibed and how they respond to a situation. In the same way, the success of any business depends upon the leadership's thought process and how the new entrants are groomed.

Summary

- *In future, many conventional industries will be impacted by technological innovation.*

- *Believing that you can do it is far different from Achieving. It is a move from "Proficiency" to "Efficiency".*

- *Your achievement in the current assignment is what you believe about yourself. It is the qualification for your next role.*

- *The industry is not aware of the skillset requirements to handle a new type of opportunities which the industries will throw open.*

- *You do not have control over your Sun of Apprehension – the external environment.*

- *You are the only one who can manage your Sun of Control – the internal environment.*

- *Always focus to enlarge your Sun of Control.*

- *The gap between the Sun of Apprehension and Sun of Control is your Area of Concern.*

- *Control of your Area of Concern will enhance your chances to succeed in life.*

Action Plan

- Write down the apprehension you face in your current assignment or life. Also, mention if you have any control over it.

  _____

  _____

- Write down how you intend to overcome these apprehensions. Also mention if the control actions are within your purview and not influenced by external factors.

  _____

  _____

- Are any specific skills required to overcome the listed apprehension?

  _____

  _____

- Are your actions in harmony with the culture and values identified?

  _____

  _____

Chapter 5

Focus on Profitability

5.1 Emerging Business

We have so many start-up companies which are valued at more than $ 1.0 billion. As per the Angel List Report, three out of four start-ups fail. Many have survived due to merger and acquisition.

Start-up companies begin with ideas. It does not require any land acquisition to start the operation. It is all in the minds of the people. The ideas are developed into concepts. The concepts need to be defined in terms of need, input, output, scalability, reach, revenue model and many other parameters. The concept must be tested as a pilot project to evaluate the possible solution which is envisaged for the identified problem. Then the market identification is done followed by the product launch. Each of these is identified as different stages of start-up operation – ideation/ concept formulation, pilot testing, market identification and then launch. Development of the framework and the processes for each stage needs to be carefully defined.

Aspects that are critical are:

- When to conduct pilot testing?

- What are the essential features necessary for pilot testing?

- Is the product ready for testing or need more features to gain traction during the testing phase?

The problem in not defining and identifying the stage of start-up will adversely impact resource allocation and its revenue model. The company may eventually run out of cash to survive. In the race to bridge this gap from concept to product launch, many companies pay very attractive salaries to retain talent, particularly to the technical team. Where salaries are low, they are adequately compensated with equity. This is because finance is available from an alternate source like venture capitalists. The success rate of getting a project financed is increasingly being decided by the number of clicks to the website rather than conventional ways. Understanding "*how business works*" is gaining more importance than the business itself.

Sustenance of such start-up companies depends upon the money being financed by various agencies. Many such companies are eventually taken over by their competitors only based valuation and not profitability. Flipkart, India's answer to Walmart, took over Myntra, an Indian fashion e-commerce company. Both companies were founded in 2007. Myntra acquired Jabong, again into fashion e-commerce retail business. Ultimately Flipkart was taken over by Walmart. Corporates are increasingly coming out with innovative means to garner market share. The launch of Reliance Jio in India changed the way, the telecom industry had worked earlier.

In 1998, Kodak sold 85% of all photo paper worldwide even though the digital camera had been invented in 1975. Interestingly the inventor of digital photography, Steven Sasson worked for Kodak. Kodak's management appreciation of the digital technology as per Sasson was *"That's cute, but don't tell anyone about it."* Kodak ignored the new technology and eventually went bankrupt. Don Strickland, former Vice President of Kodak said: *"We developed the first consumer digital camera but we could not get the approval to launch or sell it because of the fear of the effects on the film market."* It lost on both fronts. Today we hardly print photos on paper except to fill application forms. Another multinational company which failed to recognize its associated product line as disruptive technology is Nokia. It was the market leader in a cellular phone in the 1990s and early 2000. With the explosion of internet and software driving the revolution to the smartphone, it still believed in its brand strength to retain the market share. However, with the arrival of Apple in 2007, it was too late for Nokia to create an impact on the user experience of a mobile phone. Many devices which we thought would last our lifetime are no longer existing – Floppy disks, Audio/ videotapes, Typewriters, Maps, dial-up modems, Landline telephone, answering machines, pagers, dot matrix printers to name a few.

The technology revolution has even changed the concept of traditional business operation like automobile and hotel. You no longer need to invest in creating assets. Avis and Hertz earlier acquired cars, generally General Motors brands of Chevrolet or Cadillac. Even after being in operation for more than six decades, it is way behind Uber, Ola and Taxi for Sure which do not own any assets of their own to operate. Uber, Taxi for Sure and Ola are just application tools. They own very few cars and some use only hired cars on a revenue-sharing model. Yet, they are among the biggest Taxi companies in the world.

The next generation or so to say Y2K generation may even not have the necessity to own a car shortly. Many options are available now to them. One can hire cabs and self-drive. Cars are available for hire along with the driver. One can even hire luxury cars or SUVs to meet their specific needs. You also have an option to hire only drivers. The mobile application makes it convenient to book it from the comforts of your home or office. It drives you to the destination and even removes the hassles of parking and maintenance. It may eliminate the need for owning a driving license forever and still, it may not impact your life in a big way. The self-driving cars of Google and Tesla are also likely to negatively impact other sectors like insurance. Accidents rate will reduce. Google has even introduced a self-riding bicycle with advanced safety features, just as a four-wheel drive, to balance it hands-free.

The automobile industry is witnessing a revolution with technologically advanced self-driven cars made by Tesla and Google. The latest being the research in the field of nuclear batteries by a Russian scientist. It will again impact the automobile sector in the future. The nuclear batteries are designed with a half-life of 100 years. There will be no need to charge it for a century. However, it's a commercial application for the automobile as well as for the health sector needs much more acceptability by the consumers for the fear of being exposed to the radioactive material.

A similar situation has emerged in the hotel industry. Marriot, Four Seasons, Shangri La, Ritz Carlton, Taj, Oberoi etc. may still be the best brands in the hotel industry. But the newer concept of offering bed and breakfast, usage of homestay, and utilizing mid-segment hotel rooms with look and feel of luxury brands have altered the scenario. The best brands are no longer the biggest name in the hospitality sector. Airbnb is now the biggest hotel company in the world with a presence in more than 150 countries and with over 1.5 million rooms. Airbnb does not own any property. There is no requirement to invest in creating assets. OYO rooms are another home-grown Indian example of the flourishing hotel industry driven by software. Artificial Intelligence (AI) will further enhance the user experience.

AI is gaining significant importance. It has transformed the way business is being operated today. It is further impacting not only the traditional sectors but also the service industry as well as the niche industry like medicine and forensic science with high-end diagnostic tools and face recognition software. Home automation to save energy, to prevent burglaries and even to do household chores have already made their entry.

Legal advice is available with 90% accuracy at a click of a button. The world is focusing on producing cheaper electricity with the harnessing of alternative source of energy be it solar, wind, biogas etc. The banking system has seen a revolutionary change with the introduction of mobile money. 3D printing or Additive Manufacturing (AM) is going to be the next manufacturing revolution. It is now being used to manufacture rotating parts and with much greater accuracy.

Artificial Intelligence has highlighted the need to develop a good corporate culture for sustainability. The earlier management concept of pyramidal organization structure is slowly being replaced with an organizational framework which focuses more on creativity, innovation, individualism and open hierarchy. A lot of new concepts are emerging which utilizes artificial intelligence and information technology to reduce duplicity and improve productivity. It is no more viewed as a support service. It is now becoming the driving force in improving productivity and profitability. The system openness provides adequate authority at each level for effective decision making.

5.2   Business Economics[3]

Understanding of business economics is essential for day to day survival. Business economics in a true sense is a reflection of how we operate our daily lives for our livelihood. You do not need to be drowned with financial jargon.

Some components of finance, however, must be imbibed by all section of the organization. In corporate finance, a new financial analysis involves the use of Economic Value Added (EVA). EVA is Net Operating

---

[3] *The deliberations on business economics are influenced by the book " What the CEO wants you to know" by Dr Ram Charan*

Profit after Tax (NOPAT) less cost of capital. The main goal of any business operation is to increase the shareholder's value using existing resources. EVA is a financial tool for quantification and measurement of the economic value created by a business operation.

But EVA can be incorporated at every level by all the departments by following the basic components of economics-related cash flow, margin, customer and growth.

The above economic criteria are not just applicable to business. If we have a holistic view, we realize that it applies to almost every organization be it large corporate or small enterprises, government, NGO, social or religious organizations, charitable institution, an industry body, professional body etc. Everyone follows the basic concept of business for their survivability. The measurement parameters for each may be different but the principles remain the same.

5.3 Cash Flow

Cash Flow is a basic necessity for business survivability. Many companies have perished due to non-availability of cash which is essential for day to day operation. Cash is very different from income. Cash is the availability of funds in the company's account. Income is future cash availability. Timing of the money receivables affects cash availability. We must understand the importance of cash in a business. Cash availability can be held up in inventory, receivables, credit limit etc. It is also important for other organizations like government, NGO, social, religious etc.

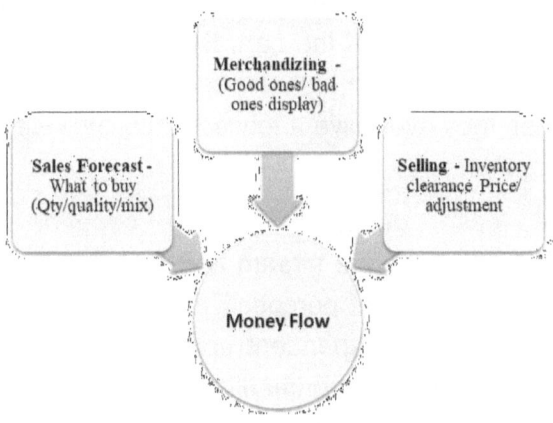

The basic business model depends upon formulating a sales forecast, merchandising and selling to generate the money flow. It applies to a big corporate as well as to a roadside vendor. When we visit a big departmental store, the product positioning is done as per its selling ability. Shelf space is provided accordingly to cater to this aspect. The sales forecast is planned to cater for the volume. Selling generates money to keep the operation going. Bananas have been the top-selling items for years in Walmart. For Amazon, technology products like play stations, Alexa, TV remote etc. are hot selling items. If we compare it with a road-side vegetable vendor, they also follow the same principle. They also do their sales forecast of what to buy, what quantity to buy and what should be the product mix based on the selling data which is in their mind. The product display is also done by them accordingly on their cart. Good quality items are stacked in front, which is constantly shuffled to maintain the attraction of the customers. Discounts are offered based on the customer so that even not so good quality products are taken off the cart. By the end of the day, they may even give a higher discount. For the regular customer, they even give a few essential ingredients as compliments.

The cash generation ability depends upon increasing the revenue stream and curtailing the cost. From the government perspective, cash generation or revenue stream is dependent upon taxes, both direct and indirect. Direct tax primarily relates to Income tax. Indirect tax relates to the excise duty, sales tax, value-added tax, customs duty, and a plethora of other taxes. The cost or expenditure of the government is related to various government schemes, infrastructure projects, the subsidy provided by the government etc. Cash generation ability will increase if the government can increase its revenue stream and curtail their expenditure. The limited revenue stream can only be increased by widening the tax net.

Even large social organizations or NGO's need to ensure the availability of cash to fund their various projects. It is done by way of donations or through Corporate Social Responsibility (CSR) activities of the big companies. The availability of cash to fund their projects depends upon its successful implementation. If the project is successful, many social organizations get matching grants from internationally funded organizations. The company spending through CSR has improved confidence in the NGOs in effective utilization of the funds provided.

In business organizations, we have sales forecasting, merchandising and selling to generate cash. For government or NGOs, it is financial planning, advertising of scheme to reach every individual and its successful implementation. Cash is necessary for any organization for its sustenance. It is important to keep track of the cash generation ability of the organization. Sales may grow but if cash generation is also not growing, future sustainability will be difficult.

5.4 Margin

Margin is the profit which the company generates. Profit is generated when goods/ services are sold. The turnaround of inventory decides how much profit we generate with the available funds. Similarly, the quality of service decides what type of Annual Maintenance Contract (AMC) will be offered and what value people will be willing to pay for the offered services. We frequently see experts evaluating various firms in terms of Return on Asset (ROA), Return on Equity (ROE), Return on Investment (ROI) and other financial ratios. These are all financial tools/ parameters to evaluate how much money the company is making as well as how efficiently it is making. There are many other parameters to evaluate the performance of an individual department.

Let's review the concept of margin from a street vendor's point of view. A street vendor buys products from the local market taking a loan at a rate of 30% per annum. The products are sold at a profit margin of just 0.5%. Few items are even sold at a discount. Do you think that the street vendor makes any profit? They certainly do. It all depends upon how quickly the inventory is turned around. If the complete cart of inventory is sold by the end of the day, every day of the month, they make a profit of 0.5% multiplied by 30 days, a whopping 15% a month. This is against 30% they pay annually on the loan. The goods are purchased daily and sold by the end of the day, even at a discount to ensure inventory turnaround.

Government and social organizations do not operate for profit. But they need to keep fiscal deficit under control. The expenditure should not overshoot revenue collection by a wide margin. In doing so, corruption is a major problem, which all organization particularly the government have to face. Funds for government schemes and programs are pilfered leading to poor project quality or its delayed implementation. The efficiency of the government or any other related organization is gauged by how quickly they can implement the schemes or complete the project which will help them in their cash generation ability. The government has addressed many of these issues, to a large extent, by enabling Direct Benefit Transfer (DBT) into the bank account of the beneficiary of various social schemes and to people who get relief under various loan waiver schemes. From the government perspective, revenue generation depends on speedy completion of infrastructure projects. It will further boost trade, revenue collection and provide a better return on asset (ROA).

5.5 Growth

For any business, growth is equally important as profitability. Identification of growth opportunities should always be on the agenda of the company. Growth strategy should keep in mind how the product line can be interfaced with AI, to give a better feel and the user experience of the product to the customer. Growth helps to build confidence in the minds of the people about the company. It helps the company to enhance its bargaining power. A company should focus on the growth of its business associates and vendors also by helping them develop cost-effective processes and passing on the cost benefits to its business associates and vendors.

Growth needs to be carefully planned. It should be done keeping in mind the focus area and core strength of the company. Constant review of business portfolios is essential to unlock value and improve stakeholders' trust. Disinvestment of non-core assets to focus on market expansion and to strengthen the existing product line is the key to success. Holding on to a weak product line or a non-core area, will not only put a financial constraint on the company but it will also dent its future profitability and sustainability.

Profitability and growth always go hand in hand. Growth is the future profitability of the company. Just as the corporate culture is the immune system of the business, growth is the nervous system of the business. Growth needs to focus on capturing the market information and transmitting it to various departments of the organization. Growth strategy should able to detect the environmental changes that may affect the organization in future. A company with no growth strategy will sure to have a nervous breakdown in future. It will go into depression seeing its competitor's growth.

Growth is essential for better talent acquisition, retention and promotion. Growth can be by organic or inorganic means. Companies need to strategize business plans keeping obsolescence, future technology, focus on the core areas, utilization of skilled manpower for more productive work etc. in mind. We see many senior executives leave their high paying jobs and join start-up companies. They see better growth opportunities for them in start-ups. They find a better opportunity to explore their talents and take leadership roles in mentoring young energetic teams.

From a business perspective, if one has to invest in a company which has a focused approach on creating additional revenue generation stream, curtailing cost, long term growth and work towards customer satisfaction, one will be happy to invest.

Personal growth and meeting individual aspirations is critical for talent retention. It applies to every sector. For example, in education, earlier the senior-most professor was designated as Head of the Department (HOD). Other professors could not get an opportunity to become HOD until the retirement of the existing HOD. Now the position has become rotational. Every professor gets an opportunity to become the HOD. It is tenure based. Individual aspirations are fulfilled. Talented teachers do not leave institutions for such a position in other institution. In some government organizations, a system of Non-Functional Upgrade has been implemented. Those who cannot be promoted due to non-availability of vacancy are compensated financially with the pay scale of the higher grade. But the positional authority is not given.

From the Indian government perspective, schemes like "Make in India", "Start-Up India", "Stand Up India", "Skill Development", aims for more inclusive growth by encouraging multinational companies to manufacture their products in India as well as to promote entrepreneurship. Growth is always a long-term assessment. It should focus on the expansion of business opportunities for future revenue generation. It decides the long-term outlook of a company and provides direction aligned to the vision of the company. It is no different for any government. The Indian government is focusing to make India a manufacturing hub for the world through various schemes and incentives. Increase in manufacturing activity will create jobs and enhancement of skills, ensuring long term growth. The government is also aware that long term benefits will accrue if they can sustain short term pains.

It is no different for any social organization or an NGO as well. For any social organization or an NGO, its visibility is the focal point. Are they expanding their activities? Are completing more and more projects? Is member enrolment on the rise? Do they have the capability to operate from multiple locations? All these enhance their credibility and people's faith in them, who contribute money. Your words will then have more value.

The growth provides an opportunity to retain talent. A person who has both self-management and business management skills is the biggest asset to any organization. Can we create more and more such people? Today, employees are focusing more on the type of work environment, social life, organization values and ethics etc. to associate themselves with an organization. It is not just remuneration. In today's business environment, retaining a good employee is the most challenging job.

5.6 Customer

The customer is the ultimate king. If an enterprise loses focus of customers, it cannot survive. They are the actual consumers of goods and services. The product and services need to be constantly upgraded to suit their likes, dislikes and preferences. Organizations offer incentives, buyback schemes, discounts, freebies etc. to ensure customer retention. Even roadside vegetable vendors offer small things free to ensure customer loyalty. Low price or good services no more can attract and retain customers. These are now essential requirements.

In earlier times, the salespersons were considered ambassadors of the company. They were the ones who would take orders and provide feedback about the customer's needs so that the products and the services can be designed to match the need of the customer. However, the penetration of internet and Artificial Intelligence has put a tremendous squeeze on the margins. Prices are low and competition is high.

On the retail side, the concept of the dealership has also undergone a phenomenal change. Call centres now play a very big role both in customer acquisition as well as their retention. Today, it is no longer about selling what you produce. It is more about meeting customer goals and priorities. It is more focused on learning consumer's insight, the knowledge of their finances, and how it relates to your offerings. The focus is not on price discounting but is more on inventory turnaround. The pace at which new products are introduced in the market has created a shelf space crunch. If you want to sell software to a retailer, you need to also convince him on how it can help in improving their operation and not just accounting. Can it flag inventory receivables? Does your supplier have compatible software? Can it help in better inventory turnaround or lower inventory management?

Today's salesperson is like a diagnostician. They need input from manufacturing, marketing, technical, IT, R&D finance and almost every department to get an insight into customer behaviour. It is no more about the low price, good quality and excellent service. It is more about collaboration and delegation. In today's scenario, if you want to be associated with a reputed company, you need to imbibe the ethos and principles of the company. Is your company's culture aligned to the organization you wish to be associated? Who are the influencers or decision-makers in the organization? How can you help in improving their process? Can you add value to the product? These are some of the questions that need deliberation.

Let's illustrate it with an example. Tata Steel is a global brand in steel manufacturing. Its present iconic advertisement campaign reads "*We also make tomorrow*". In the current situation of COVID 19 pandemic, the focus is on CSR head who interacts with the government officials, social organizations and with society at large. He is the person who is marketing the brand and helping in its image projection in line with the advertisement campaign. Today, sales head need a cross-functional team with input from varies sources to attract customers.

The best way to retain a customer or be associated with a big brand is to show them how the product or the services offered can help in increasing cash flow, improving margin, leading to continued growth and customer retention. Interpersonal relationship, technologically superior products, low pricing in comparison to competitors or better ROI based on the offered pricing cannot guarantee an order. For this, it is essential to understand how the organization conducts its business operation and makes money. You may have a better chance of winning a customer and retaining it if you focus on customer's SWOT (Strength Weakness Opportunities and Threats) analysis rather than your own.

From the government perspective, rural India is the largest customer base. They are the one who votes them to power. Intellectuals only debate on television. Rural India exercises its franchise – their right to vote. Urban India is now coming in large numbers to vote. Voting day is no more just a holiday. It is acquiring the glamour of festivity. Customer satisfaction is also ensured by providing better infrastructure particularly to rural India, direct bank transfer of money to their bank account, better health care, electricity, drinking water, sanitation, insurance, pensions and other schemes, which enhances their standard of living. The focus is shifting from *Ease of Doing Business* to *Ease of Living*.

Summary

- *Artificial intelligence is the next level of technological change which will be witnessed by mankind.*

- *Business sustainability requires an understanding of*

- *Business economics – Management of the current financial situation*

- *Maintaining a good corporate culture – for future sustainability*

- *Understanding of Cash Flow, Margin, Customer and Growth is essential for organizational sustainability.*

Action Plan

- Write down five work areas which can be improved with innovation and use of technology.

  _____

  _____

- Identify five work areas where the business economy needs to be improved.

  _____

  _____

- Identify training needs required to address the business and technology challenges.

  _____

  _____

SECTION IV – PRACHAAR

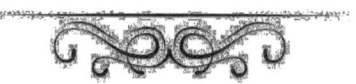

Chapter 6

Leadership in Today's Scenario

The transparency brought into the system by digital transformation has opened the most debatable question of integrity and trust. Biswajeet Bhattacharya, former Attorney General of India once remarked: *"Profits are privatized but losses are nationalized"*. Most discussions today relate to the building of trust among the people. Leadership needs to address the issue of trust and integrity with utmost sincerity and honesty. The biggest challenge being faced by companies is to develop and communicate this trust, both, within the organization and to society at large through effective leadership. This leads to the aspect of Prachaar.

6.1 Evolving Leadership Model

If we evaluate the leadership model using a two by two matrix, the following can be deduced

A true leader is an influencer. He acquires the leadership position by displaying very high values. He commands authority since he leads by setting a personal example. All of us aspire to be in this position (quadrant No. 2). A leader always maintains a balance between self and the outside world. His senses and perception powers are more alive and active.

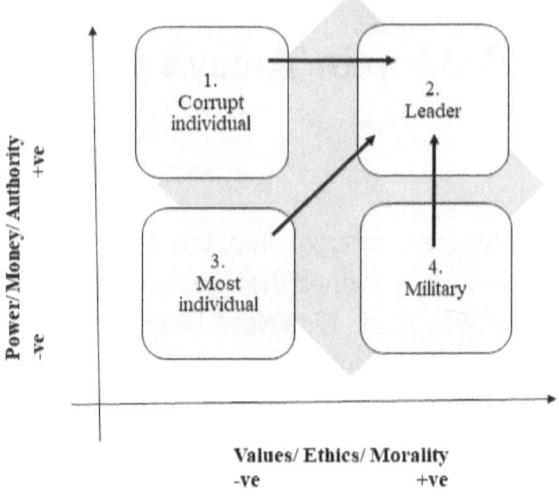

In ancient India, there were many Rishis (a sage). Many of these rishis go into a state of Samadhi (a *state of deep meditative contemplation which leads to higher consciousness – Collins English Dictionary*). Samadhi... means maintaining a balance of mind where the external environment does not affect you. It is a state to explore yourself. In the state of samadhi, you are also able to enhance your sensory power to connect with the external cosmos to gain knowledge. Similarly, a true leader is always able to sense the feelings of the people around. His emotional connect with the people has the biggest influence in their behaviour and action.

In most cases, when people join an organization, they fall in the bottom left quadrant No.3. They neither have power, authority nor money to influence people who are decision-makers. But they all aspire to acquire it. They want greater acceptance within the society and want to be adjudged as the one holding very high moral standards and values. They want to be seen as leaders. However, it is pertinent to understand that the transition to becoming a leader is an inclined climb. The values are often compromised as they move up to maintain a balance between authority and morality. Many of them become favourite of seniors because of their ability to handle unforeseen situations.

On the other hand, we also have a certain section of inherently corrupt people. They gain money, power and authority through illegitimate means and quickly climb to quadrant No.1. Once they gain such a position, they want a larger footprint in society by projecting themselves as ideal individuals portraying that they care for society, environment and others even at the expense of their sufferings. Such people seek straight horizontal transition from the position of power to the position of high moral ground.

In the military, every individual is grounded to maintain high values from the initial stages of training. The importance of culture, heritage, human life, integrity and service before self in ingrained in the early stages of their career. The penalty for deviating from such principles are often very high and harsh. That is why all military leaders are always idolized and looked up to with great respect and trust at the time of crisis. It is not that military leaders never falter. Few of them fumble and succumb to external pressures to serve self before others. But most of them can do it only during the later stages of their career when they reach a position of authority. The strong foundation of military personnel in the early and middle stages of their career always helps them in maintaining uprightness which ensures them to be worthy leaders. In the military, those who constantly display high values are often promoted to leadership positions. Their transition is vertically upward – from quadrant No.4 to No.2.

If we examine this perspective moving from the individual to the organizational point of view, the matrix can be redrawn. Every organization aims to become a sustainable organization. However, the parameters of a sustainability model are seeing a shift in priorities. It now needs an amalgamation of business, care for society, community development and leadership with a focus on the resilience of the organization to continue to deliver the desired outcome in future also.

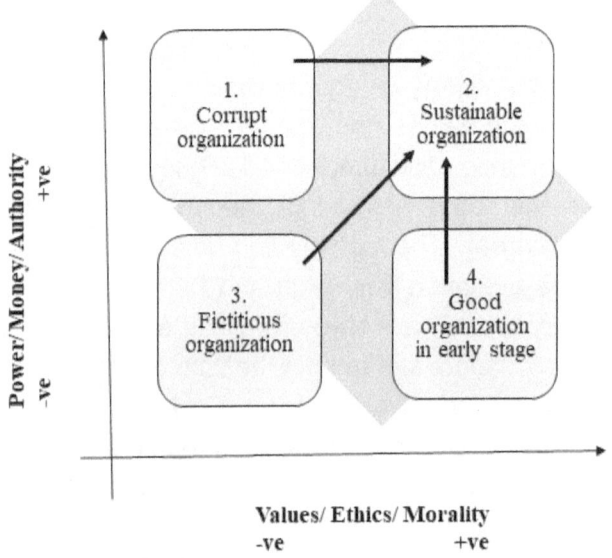

Today, the organization focus is beyond profitability. Rebuilding the lost credibility is a herculean task. It will not only impact current business prospects but also compromise its future earning capability. To ensure the future viability of an organization and its resilience to deliver the desired output in future, leadership will have to build a value-based positive character to generate goodwill in society.

Let us examine the evolving leadership model with that of the military leadership model.

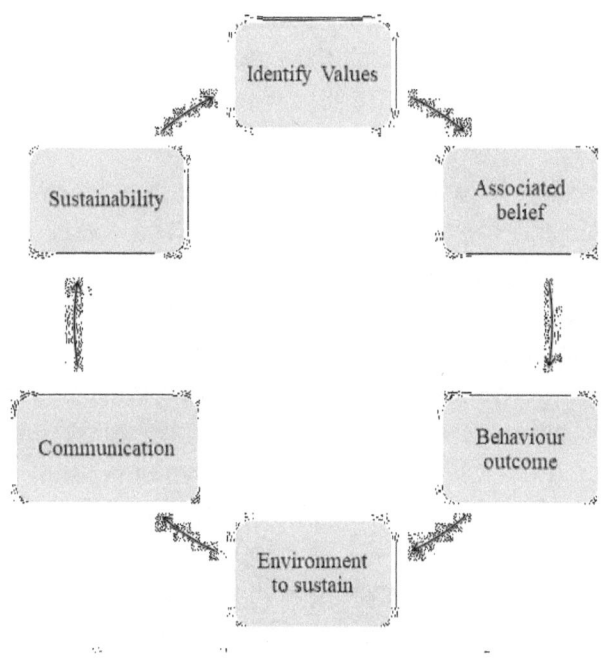

Military behaviour model – my perspective

Let us define a value, say non-adultery from a military outlook. Adultery may be acceptable in other organizations. However, in the military, it is a serious crime. In the Indian Armed Force, it is called "*Stealing the affection of a brother officer's wife*". The belief associated is – it may create discontentment among the soldiers. The level of trust will be drastically affected if such a value is compromised, since, soldiers spend considerable time away from the family. They expect brotherhood and bonhomie to be exercised and maintained. The behavioural outcome may vary though. It could lead to very serious repercussion since a soldier is armed, which if not assessed and corrected, can even lead to loss of life. How do we control this behaviour?

Creation of a healthy environment is essential to maintain the trust level and goodwill. The focus is to increase the happiness quotient. Severe punishment is imposed, leading to discharge from service that too with disgrace. In such a condition, a soldier not only loses his pension but is also barred from consideration to any other government job. Communication plays an important role. Many feedback systems exist for continuous assessment of the behaviour of a soldier to maintain a high level of happiness quotient. The outcome is a happy environment, where, a soldier has an elated level of trust and is willing to perform his duty without any apprehensions. This leads to a sustainable organization.

Let us examine the military leadership model with a framework from the industry's perspective.

Most people join the Armed Force, not for money considerations but the honour attached to it. There are instances where you will find a member or members from each generation within families being a part of the Indian Military. It becomes a family culture and tradition for some and they take pride in this heritage. There are also cases where the only two professions considered honourable by residents of a village is either joining the military or agriculture. It is their enduring preference. In all such cases, the individual's value system is already aligned to the Armed Force's value system. Once a person joins the Military, the individual's value system needs fortification to embed the same in their character, which gets reflected in their personality. The organizational value system is further reinforced during training and personal interaction. That is why, when a soldier interacts with the society at large, their behaviour and character also reflect the same aspiration – to serve. The organizational framework is also created to continuously succour this aspect. The value alignment helps in forging and developing a good corporate culture. This helps in the intermingling of the belief system of the individual with the organization to get a positive behavioural outcome in tune with organizational culture. The leadership at the helm should exploit this behaviour to build an effective relationship with the communities and societies/ environment it operates including all stakeholders in the value chain. A feedback system will ensure the closure of the loop to build a sustainable model.

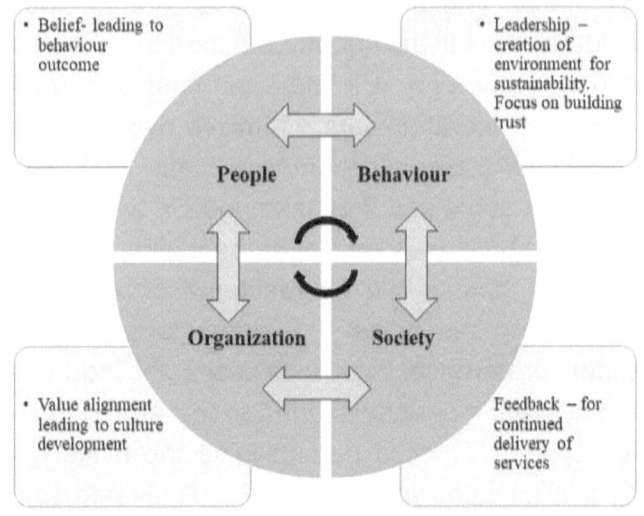

Military leadership model – my perspective

6.2 IT Revolution and Age of Start-Up in India

Today Start-Ups are gaining momentum. The government has focused more on creating a sustainable model to support start-ups. The spotlight is on Innovation, Creativity and Technology. Global Innovative Index (GII) is a ranking of countries as per their success and capacity in innovation. The index is published by the World Intellectual Property Organization (WIPO). In 2017, India has been ranked as the 57th most innovative nation in the world among 126 nations. It has emerged as the most innovative nation among Central and South Asian countries. Emphasis has been laid on human resource capital, Research & Development (R&D), knowledge creation, knowledge impact and knowledge diffusion through Information and Communication Technology (ICT) infrastructure, regulatory framework, the ease of getting investment, creativity in service and online content management. Incubation centres have been set up in universities/ Institutions. Tinkering labs have been established in schools to promote innovation and creativity and support R&D at the early stage itself.

It is believed that future market competition will be dominated by Artificial Intelligence. Three decades earlier, information was power. With Right to Information (RTI Act) and availability of information online, information is no more considered power or knowledge but is now merely a data. Data Analytics has changed our idea of information and its ways of interpretation. Today, Data Analytics is being used for market studies related to competition, size, and segmentation, understanding customer likes and dislikes, investment availability and even to win an election. Processing data helps to convert data into knowledge. Technology and knowledge (processed data) are hence pillars of innovation and invention.

As per KPMG report, 50000 start-ups are working in India in 2018, up 7.4 times since 2008. The Ministry of Commerce and Industry in India has recognized 15667 start-ups till Jan 19, as per the tweet by the Minister Mr Suresh Prabhu. The growth in a start-up is also fuelled by the availability of funds through alternate sources particularly Venture Capital funding. As per the business newspaper Livemint report, in the first half of 2019, Start-ups raised more than USD 3.9 billion in funding. The investment in start-ups in the first half of

2019 is comparable to complete full-year investment in 2016 and 2017. Venture Intelligence, a start-up data tracker, mentions that USD 2.7 billion was received by start-ups in funding in the first half of 2018. This is a significant jump.

We are talking about the growth of start-ups which mostly operate from big cities in India like Mumbai, Bangalore, Delhi, Hyderabad, Gurgaon, Noida etc. As per estimates, more than 4000 start-ups are being registered every year. The focus is shifting towards Tier II and Tier III cities like Jaipur, Ahmedabad, Indore, Ranchi, Patna, Kochi and other cities. In a short period, India has secured 5th place in the world in the number of start-ups by 2019. First being the USA. It is only behind, Britain, Canada and Israel. The reason for this sudden jump is government initiative, funding through Venture Capitalists (VCs), support of R&D centres and institutes where incubation centres support is provided. People often join as mentors for guiding various start-ups. Government ecosystem in terms of self-certification of labour and environmental compliance laws, Income tax exemption, rebate and support in filing patents, winding up of a company under Insolvency and Bankruptcy Code (IBC), Support via Incubator/ Mentorship program and many more such schemes has given a tremendous boost to Start-ups in India.

But despite these, many start-ups fail. A report by IBM Institute for Business Value and Oxford Economics stated that more than 90 per cent Indian start-ups fail within the first five years. Lack of innovation and funding are the main reasons. This has also contributed to unemployment among young people. However, the USD 16 billion acquisition of Flipkart by Walmart has raised the VC firm's conviction in India. Flipkart investors made healthy returns and it has increased the confidence in an Indian start-up. VC funds are now even evaluating B2B models rather than focusing only on the consumer segment or retail industry.

There are 18 Unicorn in India as of 2019. Unicorn is a company with a valuation of over USD 1billion. It is estimated that another 30 will become Unicorns by 2020. Some of the most successful start-ups in India are, Paytm, Zomato, OYO, Ola, Swiggy, BookMyShow, Byjus, Snapdeal, Shopclues, policy bazaar etc. The valuation of these 10 start-ups adds up to nearly USD 46 Billion (*Source – Economic Times 04*th *Oct 19 and Wikipedia*). Despite funding, one of the biggest challenges faced by these start-ups is mentorship. India is a multicultural and multilingual society.

Creating a revenue stream is easy but sustaining it is an arduous task. Start-up founders are relatively young. They have great ideas which need good mentorship and nurturing to survive in the Indian ecosystem. The problem will be further compounded by the present pandemic COVID19. The dependency of local retailers has increased during this period. It would now require a model where local retailers are also part of the e-commerce system. The footfall in big shopping retail centres will be impacted due to fear of pandemic. This new societal normal will put pressure on revenue stream and many more start-ups are likely to fail. In such a condition, winning the trust of the people will emerge as the winning strategy and not by giving freebies due to delay in delivery etc. The cultural background of people will also play a role.

The start-ups' mentorship will have to focus on developing a belief system within the organization which would be reflected in the employee's behaviour. Only then the leadership can win the trust of the people.

6.3   Call for Leadership in Today's Environment

Under the circumstances, what kind of leadership is required to guide the current generation to ensure the survivability of any organization in future? Most leadership theories focus on leadership traits and style. In the present context, when the world is witnessing a pandemic of a different kind affecting both the conduct and outcome of the business, leadership needs to focus on five aspects. All five aspects must address the facet of VAP to meet the challenges of the current digitization age.

- Building character
- Value-based learning
- Role model
- Develop an attitude of gratitude
- Maintain equanimity with nature

The initial two factors relate to value and cultural development, which shapes our conviction and regulate our behaviour. The last three factors press on leadership and its interface with society. This will assess and reflect the limits, which when breached, will impact the relationship between each of the VAP elements.

6.3.1 Building Organization Character

We all start our life with a family, the mother being the core member responsible for bringing stability within the family. Destroying the core will ensure the failure of the entire system. It is this very mother who creates and nurtures future leaders and instils the first lessons of value systems in her children. If she falters, the next generation will suffer. Her contribution has a futuristic impact. Hence, her role is extremely crucial which should be revered and acknowledged by all.

Same is the case with teachers. A relation between a student and a teacher is often compared to that of a devotee and god. Such is the kind of respect teachers deserve. If the students look down upon their teachers, or parents start to question their integrity, the education system is demolished. A student's role model gets lowered. If we list down ten people who have impacted our lives in the most significant way, mothers and teachers will invariably appear in the list. The day we weaken their position, there will be no one left to teach us the importance of values, ethics and morality in our lives. Future civilization will crumble and will eventually perish.

The Chinese had built The Great Wall of China thinking nobody could invade them which could let them live in peace. But unfortunately, they were invaded more than once. On each occasion, invaders did not need to go through the trouble of tiding over the wall, but they gained access by easily bribing the guards.

Organization culture is hence the foundation on which the character is built. For a nation, its people are its family. For a corporate, the employees are its family. If you do not put your heart and soul in building the character of the employees, then few unscrupulous employees will easily be able to deceive the organization and bring disrepute to it.

Character building is a complex and a long-drawn process. Apart from professionalism, it should build a sense of heritage, give hope, optimism and bring resilience among the people. Two components are critical while building a positive culture and character of the organization.

The first aspect deals with Mentorship (*Mentorship means... the activity of giving a younger or less experienced person help and advice over some time, especially at work or school... Cambridge dictionary*). Mentorship is to provide active guidance to the people to influence their thinking in the right direction. Mentorship is not only about guidance. It is also about Listening. It gives an insight into people thought process which is an important aspect in determining their behaviour. In Sanskrit, mentor means *Margdarshak − a guide*. He is the person who gives direction to our life. He understands our belief system, moulds it to suit a behaviour outcome which is more acceptable to meet the challenges of life. He is more than an advisor on business matters. He lifts us when we are down and out. He is the cheerleader for our life who helps us to be happy.

Mentors, who stick through difficult phases and ensure their mentee has attained success, are always fondly and respectfully remembered. We may have mentors at our respective educational institutions or in our families. However, in our professional career, it somehow gets side-lined. We fail to create the second rung of leadership. Many a time, we are influenced by wrong role models whose negative tendencies seem to impact our behaviour. Before mentoring someone, one must ask the basic question about our behaviour which may influence our juniors – Who has the greatest positive influence in our lives and why? What characteristics of the individual one would like to imbibe and why? How should one improve to become a role model for others?

Charlie Kim is the CEO of Next Jump – a tech company in the US. In his company, nobody loses the job on performance issues. Kim believes that if you had a hard time in your family, would you consider laying off one of your children? You would never do it. Then why do we do it inside our organization? In Next Jump, if you have a performance issue, they coach you, mentor you but not fire you. If you feel safe and protected by the organization, your trust and loyalty of the organization increases.

The second aspect deals with taking pride in our heritage and its projection. People not only evaluate you for your professionalism but they also assess you all the time for your sense of heritage. The heritage is a reflection of the cultural values imbibed by an organization over some time. It needs to be preserved, protected and respected. It is the self-esteem of the organization. The behaviour outcome will be vastly different if you have low self-esteem about the organization you are working for. It is also equally important to make it noticeable to others. You must make sure that people see that you take pride in your heritage. Only then they will emulate you.

All the above components are critical to building a good character for the organization. Always remember that people want to follow you. But, the question is, are you displaying the qualities which you want others to emulate?

6.3.2 Value-Based Learning

In the corporate world, it is believed that an employee is saved when the organization has improved, or when it makes money. In the military, it is believed that when a soldier is improved, the organization is saved. The focus is on the person who delivers to the organization. Hence, every effort is made to build the character of the person in line with the organization.

Today, more and more organization are adopting an unconventional approach to hire people. It could be by solving case studies, internship, hiring on contract and making them understand the practical difficulties of the role before confirming. It allows them to understand the behavioural aspect of the recruit. Will he/she fit in our culture? It is similar to military recruitment, which we talked in the earlier chapter.

Learn the Value of Things and Not Its Price

At an alumnus meet, a student met his favourite teacher after many years. The teacher, however, couldn't recognize him. The teacher inquired, "What do you do?" The student replied, "You have been the biggest source of my inspiration. I am now a teacher, just as you are." The teacher got curious and asked, "How did I inspire you?" The student narrated an incident, "In our class, one student had brought an expensive pen. Since I could not afford it, I stole it and kept it in my pocket. The friend later realized that his expensive pen has been stolen. He complained to you. You closed the door. You asked every student to stand in line with eyes closed. I felt ashamed that I will be caught. You started checking everybody's pocket. You got the pen from my pocket and gave it to the student to whom it belonged. You never told anybody that it was me who stole the pen. Neither did you ever called and talked to me about my misbehaviour. You upheld my dignity. I realized what a teacher is and I decided to become one." "Now do you remember me?" the student inquired. "No", replied the teacher, "because I too had closed my eyes while I was checking."

Author Unknown

Germany is probably the only country, where primary school teachers are paid the highest. It is believed that people who teach you the right attitude, make you conduct responsibly and teach you "*How to live*" must be paid more than the students, who may or may not imbibe the same. Teaching is the only profession which creates other professions. Recognition of people who make a difference in your attitude at an early stage is very important. This is so true, as we may not remember the name of the most successful person, we have interacted with but we certainly remember the name of our school teacher who may have made a huge impact on our minds while growing. We certainly value that much more in our private life but may not do so in our public life. But for a Nation to change, this thinking has to change.

Value-based learning is a continuous process. Educating people on areas of concern doesn't always need an emphasis on a negative situation. If you always give an example of a negative situation, negativity is all that will be absorbed. If you want a behavioural change to inculcate a sense of success in them, then they need to see more of good than bad. Discussion on failure stories always gives impetus to lessons learnt. But success stories always reflect on how success can be achieved. It is essential to understand the impact you create on your staff through your leadership style.

Your subordinates are always watching you. Are you also displaying right tendencies with your superior the way you expect from your juniors? Let us see an example of value-based learning which has a positive influence on leadership style in the current situation.

For over 125 years, Coke dominated the beverage market across the world. It even changed its product line to suit the current environment where people are more health-conscious and now offer more than 180 products which are low calorie or zero-calorie. It realized that in a growing society dominated by technology, it needs to make people aware of a certain fact, which may not be in its business interest. But it certainly was in the interest of the people and the country at large. So it came out with a campaign highlighting the adverse effect of drinking coke. It was a bold campaign. The campaign highlighted that drinking excessive coke could increase your chances of heart disease, stroke, diabetes, obesity and cancer. Calories in coke have no nutritional value. If one wants to live a healthy lifestyle, then they should not drink coke. The advertisement ends with *"We are partially responsible for America's obesity problem."* How many companies can do such a campaign?

At a very young age, we are all groomed to become an engineer, doctor, police officer, professional, businessmen etc. The focus is always on acquiring knowledge, competency and skill in the area where we want to excel. But nobody teaches us how to use our acquired knowledge for the benefit of society. The focus needs to be shifted from *"What* we *want to become"* to *"how we can contribute to society"*. Only then can we create an environment to imbibe value-based learning. Let me amplify this with a living example of an extraordinary person.

He was rejected by 17 universities.

He became a hacker

He was ranked No.1 in Hackerone 2015

He hacked more than 400+ websites including Google, Facebook, Microsoft, Twitter

He made millions by reporting bugs to top-notch technology companies

Later, he started his venture

His focus – Improve cybersecurity of the world. Make it more secure and safe.

Now he travels the world giving seminars on cybersecurity

He is the CEO of Veiliux

His company helps the organization to secure their online business

His name is Shahmeer Amir

He is a Pakistani national.

6.3.3 Role Model

Having role models in our lives is important. He is the one, who leads by example, thereby focusing on the positive aspects of leadership, with a vision to create a culture, which pushes for professional and personal growth. A role model is about demonstrating passion with compassion. With trust and loyalty, a role model can show compassion when one needs assistance. People must be made to feel that they are valued. Invest your time in people so that they feel confident to confide in you, at the time of crisis.

While I was having a discussion with a group of friends on leadership, I asked them to list the qualities they feel are required to be a leader. Some of the qualities, which most of them said and agreed are depicted below.

The best role model one can come across is a mother. She is responsible to create future leaders who will go on to govern society. Mothers are the finest example to emulate as a role model. She has a goal for her children. She adjusts to the changing financial conditions to meet the goals ensuring that the cash flow is not disturbed. She can communicate most effectively with all family members even if she does not understand any language other than her native language. She leads her team from the front, makes sacrifices, put in extra hours to meet commitments and creates reserve fund for future contingencies etc.

In a democratic society as a whole, the powers are vested with the four pillars of democracy namely judiciary, media, executive and legislature. In today's democratic setup, most of these people who have the responsibility, power and authority are viewed as corrupt by the general mass. Despite the above, people still have faith in the judiciary. However long-drawn and tiring the wait maybe, judicial recourse is still viewed as one where justice will be served and where the aggrieved will get respite and relief. In today's time, the medical fraternity who are entrusted with saving lives is also eyed with suspicion. People approach doctors with mixed feelings – of trust, faith and fear, of hope and enmity, suspecting them of fleecing rather than treating them. But within changing times, and in a pandemic situation like COVID 19, they seem to be the only hope.

The only organization which has continued to garner the sympathy, trust, loyalty of the general mass and which is still considered as the last pillar of support and fall back is the Armed Forces. It is viewed as the perfect role model for any society. What makes the armed forces so special? How is character building done in Armed forces which continue to deliver time and again? Is there something for the corporate to imbibe from this culture which has stood the test of time?

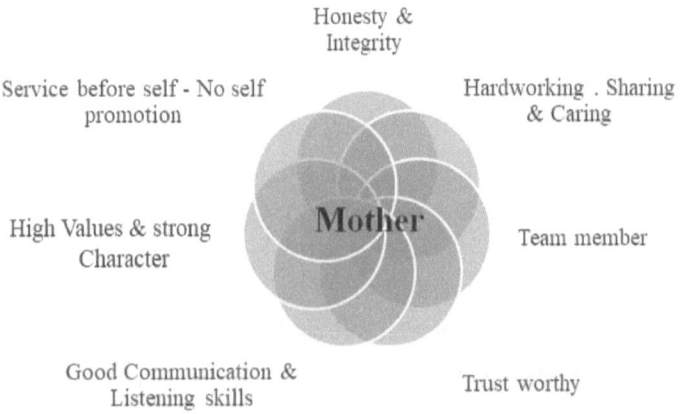

Honesty & Integrity

Service before self - No self promotion

Hardworking . Sharing & Caring

High Values & strong Character

Mother

Team member

Good Communication & Listening skills

Trust worthy

Credo of Indian Military Academy (IMA)

"The Safety, Honour, and Welfare of the Country comes first, always and every time.

The Honour, Welfare and Comfort of the men you command come next

Your Ease, Comfort and Safety come last, always and every time."

In the Armed forces, the soldier's family plays the biggest motivating role. In my experience, I have never come across any family member of the soldier perturbed while the soldier (their loved one) is sent on combat duty. They send him/ her with a sense of pride. For them, the family structure is always stable. The families of armed force personnel believe that their seniors and the head of the armed forces will always be there to support them. At the same time, every soldier's contribution is acknowledged, respected and due credit is given, by the seniors/heads leading them. The role models in armed forces are not always officers. People take pride in every soldier and many are role models for generations to come. They live forever.

A Dead Soldier Still Influences the Troops

Riflemen Jaswant Singh of the Indian Army is the only soldier, possibly in the entire world, who has continued to get unofficial promotion even after his death. He continued to rise through his ranks and is now considered to be a Major General, although he was martyred during Sino Indian War in 1962 in the battle of Nuranang, now in Arunachal Pradesh in India. He was awarded Mahavir Chakra posthumously, the second-highest gallantry award by the Indian government. There various folklore about his bravery. Local folklore says that Jaswant Singh was helped by two Monpa girls named Sela and Nura. Both kept positioning the guns at different locations to give an impression that a full platoon is fighting. The battle went on for 3 days. It was only when Nura was captured while supplying ration to the post that the Chinese realized that only one person was fighting. This infuriated them very much. Sela was killed. Jaswant Singh killed himself with the last remaining bullet before getting captured by the Chinese. The pass is named after the girl "Sela Pass".

It is believed that the Chinese, beheaded him and carried his head as a trophy because he alone fought against them which resulted in 300 Chinese casualties. The Chinese Commander was very impressed with his bravery. After the ceasefire, The Chinese commander returned the head along with a brass bust of Jaswant Singh. The brass bust, made in China by Chinese, to honour an Indian soldier is now installed at the post and the area is called Jaswant Garhi. A memorial has been erected which now has become a temple.

Today, his shrine is protected round the clock by Garhwal Rifles soldiers. A soldier cooks for him daily, makes his bed, irons his clothes, and *polishes his boots. For them, He remains immortal and continues to protect them in this difficult terrain.*

If we just replace the word country with organization and men with employees in the IMA credo, does it have relevance to the corporate? Will it create trust in the leadership and will it get more cooperation from employees? I am sure it will. We only have to follow the letter and spirit of what is written.

If you inculcate the habit among the top management to look after the employees, they will deliver what is required by you. Emotional intelligence plays a very important role in projecting yourself as well as for others to perceive you as a role model. You can perceive, understand, regulate and transmit your emotions to promote emotional and intellectual growth. Control on emotions helps in injecting the potential power of feelings into our reasoning and decision-making ability. It helps in discerning what is important or what is required to be done from what is right or wrong. It helps to maintain a sense of balance and not deviate from the values of the organization.

6.3.4   Developing an Attitude of Gratitude

We all usually take things for granted in our lives, be it the food we eat, the schools we go, friends we play with, paycheque we receive, the relationships we build etc. The situations being faced globally due to COVID 19, has brought in humility and taught people to be grateful for little basic things in life. Many of us now feel obliged towards people who just serve us a delicious meal, spend time with us playing a board game, or just call us to enquire about our well-being.

When we say "Thank You", it enhances our happiness. It gives us a sense of joy and helps us in re-living those happy moments which has a lasting effect on our mood. It motivates us to do good and better in life. Many countries have war memorials just to express their gratitude to the fallen soldiers who died for their freedom. It is time, we also have memorials for underprivileged people, doctors, nurses, health workers, police, security personnel and host of other people and communities who has stood by us in times of such crisis to fight this pandemic and to keep our life engine running. A feeling of gratitude to these people will always remind us of the importance of their contribution to our lives. People should inculcate a habit of writing a gratitude journal. Appreciating the contribution of others expands our horizon to recognize and enjoy small pleasures in life.

Let me share an incident which was narrated to me by a veteran. An officer had retired from the Indian Army after serving in the short service commission for five years. That was almost two decades back. During the present COVID 19 pandemic, he got a call from the Ex-Servicemen Directorate of the Army enquiring about his well-being and support needed, if any. The officer was working with paramilitary forces and was deployed in the interiors of the north-eastern state of India. He expressed his gratitude for such a gesture and requested to make enquiries about his family, who were staying in the western part of India. He was very amazed that the Indian Army still remembered him during such a crisis. He was equally amazed as to how the Army could locate him even after leaving the organization almost two decades back. The goodwill which such a gesture generated cannot be replaced by any other means.

6.3.5 Maintain Equanimity with Nature

There is always a debate about the human's interference with the environment. We are blessed with a variety of ecosystem and biodiversity provided by nature. It is up to us to maintain the balance of this ecosystem and biodiversity if we want to derive its benefits in future. All future decisions will have to be governed taking a holistic approach to the ecosystem and the environment we live in. COVID19 pandemic has taught the people the importance of not breaching the resilience – the ability (both in terms of capability and capacity) of the ecosystem to continue to provide the required services in future. If the ecosystem is harmed, it will cause irreparable damage to future generations.

The Indian Vedic Philosophy gives tremendous importance to the ecosystem we live in. Many things in the Indian ecosystem were and even now are considered sacred. They are treated with utmost respect and reverence – rivers, trees, plants, animals, birds etc.

The nature, type and scale of natural calamities witnessed by the world have made people realize that the time has come to recognize the importance of the natural capital and the ecosystem services we get out of it. It is important to identify and assess the benefits, which the organization derives out of this and incorporate the same in the decision-making process.

Self-aware people can perform better. A higher state of receptivity can be achieved through mediation, yoga or by observing our body and decoding the signals, it gives us. The same is valid for the environment and ecosystem we live in. We only need to be alive of its importance in our lives. Let me illustrate it with an example. Rally for the river was a national movement to save rivers in India – a drive initiated by Sadguru's Isha Foundation on 03 September, 2017. It brought into focus the importance of rejuvenating our rivers. The movement created tremendous public awareness about the importance of planting trees to rejuvenate our rivers – how trees reduce flood and droughts, how it increases farm income, how it prevents soil erosion and improve soil quality etc. Few of the facts highlighted during the movement are –

- 25% of India is turning into a desert.
- In 15 years, we may have only half the water we need for our survival.
- Estimates say that 65% of our water needs are met by the rivers.
- 2 out of 3 major Indian cities already deal with major water shortages.
- We consume water not just for drinking but about 80% of water is used to grow food.

The invisibility of the natural capital in our lives should not be seen as a hindrance in understanding its importance. The significance of biodiversity surrounding us and its co-relation with our economy and human well-being should never be under-valued. It must be recognized and respected to ensure our future prosperity.

Today's and future leaders need to recognize this aspect. Long term sustainability of any organization can only be ensured if we recognize the value which we derive from this natural ecosystem. For example, deforestation is one of the biggest problems faced by the world. This causes loss of biodiversity, increases green-house gas emissions, disrupts the water cycle, increases soil erosion and depletes the natural beauty of the surrounding area. With so many ill effects arising from it, our future generation will suffer drastic consequences, if left unchecked.

6.4   Challenges Ahead – COVID 19

Dealing with corruption was the biggest challenge faced by the world in economic prosperity. The black economy was a parallel economy which affected a nation's growth and effective utilization of the resources. Today, it is a different scenario. The world is hit by a pandemic- COVID19. Apart from the impact on the economy, it has also immensely affected our behaviour. Another challenge faced by everyone and at all levels is the circulation of fake news and countering people who propagate negative thinking. It may be called as Infodemic, which is no less dangerous than the present pandemic.

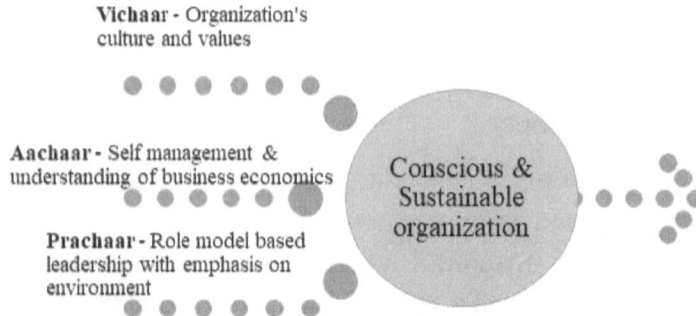

COVID 19 has re-emphasized the importance of culture, an urgency to respect the environment and expressing gratitude. The lockdown of the country has made every individual realize that in times of crisis, it is the people at the bottom of the pyramid, who even though are more stressed than many others, are our real saviours and heroes.

Currently, there are no management books, theories, or algorithms existing today to deal with such a pandemic situation. The need to balance lives and livelihood would involve enhancing the immune system of every individual as well as society as a whole. This can be done by focusing on our culture, our values, our heritage, our spiritual beliefs, and by having a positive outlook to face the challenges of life. It needs rebuilding society on a conscious foundation – being aware of the environment and mindful of human well-being. In a nutshell, it would require to imbibe the principles of *Vichaar Aachaar and Prachaar* (**VAP**)

The concept of Vichaar focuses on values and culture. But it also emphasizes on one very important aspect – that of self-awareness. The lack of self-awareness leads to loss of confidence, which creates fear in our minds. This becomes the primary source of unwanted thoughts in our minds, which disturbs our inner peace. COVID-19 has taught human beings what they are capable of. It has built an alert mind and not just a busy mind. There are numerous cases of people travelling hundreds of kilometres just to reach their homes or be with their loved ones. In a normal situation, they wouldn't have dared to take such a plunge. But just the thought to survive pushed them to test their endurance to fight back. It taught us the importance of self-introspection and positive attitude – the disciplining of mind to respond to the outside world. Just as poverty ends only when we grow rich, our problem with life can only end once we identify our inner selves through positive thoughts. That is the beginning of building a good culture and value system.

The concept of Aachaar focuses on human behaviour. It is linked to Vichaar since every action originates as an impulse in our thoughts. Human behaviour is controlled by their relationship with nature, with another man and with self. This relationship is always manifested as a conflict – which is the source of their sufferings. If you can manage the conflict with self, the other two conflicts with nature and another person can be controlled. We need to understand that our sufferings can also be a blessing in disguise. It can positively mould our behaviour. A woman is aware of the sufferings of the labour pain which she has to undergo while giving birth to a child. But the fulfilment of being a mother overcomes her sufferings. She is willing to endure the pain. COVID-19 pandemic has taught us to overcome and manage our inner conflicts or anxieties. Since money is important for human survival, the concept of Aachaar also emphasizes on money management. Money provides us with conveniences in life, which is important for survivability.

The concept of Prachaar focuses on leadership and the organization's relationship with the environment. Our life is governed by our experiences. The quality of life depends upon the type of experience we have in our life. It can improve our confidence and will-power or can weaken our resolve based on our experience. It is same for any organization. If an organization wants to survive in the future, if it wants its people to enjoy a good life, if it wants to be in harmony with nature and society, then the leadership must focus on disseminating the organization's values both within and outside the organization. It is essential to build this trust. With strong trust, we can have mutual respect for individuals, nature and society.

Summary

- *The current industrial revolution is fuelled by start-ups. Innovation & creativity are the change drivers fuelled by Artificial Intelligence.*

- *Corruption is the biggest bane plaguing the country.*

  - *Leadership in today's environment requires to focus on.*

  - *Building character*

  - *Value-based learning*

  - *Role model*

  - *Developing an attitude of gratitude*

  - *Maintain equanimity with nature*

- *Character building needs emphasis on mentorship and taking pride in heritage.*

- *Value-based learning needs emphasis in providing the same opportunity to others through positive leadership, proper education and communication.*

- *An individual should focus on how to contribute to society and not on what to become.*

- *A role model must learn to have control over his emotions. It helps in discerning what is important or what is required to be done from what is right or wrong. It helps in maintaining a sense of balance and not deviate from the values of the organization.*

- *Expressing gratitude helps in training our minds to appreciate the contribution of others in expanding our horizon to recognize and enjoy small pleasures in life.*

- *Long term sustainability of any organization can only be ensured if we recognize the value which we derive from this natural ecosystem and ensure that it continues to deliver the flow of services.*

- *COVID-19 pandemic has revealed many facets of human interaction and there is increasing realization among people to display compassion and demonstrate gratitude for whatever we get or have achieved in life.*

Action Plan

- Write down five work areas which are prone to information theft.

  _____

  _____

- Write the regulatory framework of your organization to tackle corruption.

  _____

  _____

- How are the training/ communication focused to address the core issue of Corporate Values?

  _____

  _____

- Write five instances where you have set a personal example for others to emulate.

  _____

  _____

- Identify five people who can be the role model other than senior management.

  _____

  _____

- Write your gratitude journal.

  _____

  _____

About the Author

Commander Sanjeev Raman's diverse background is the foundation of his work. Having worked in varied sectors, he believes that cutting the process complexities and empowering people is the key to success. After graduating in Metallurgical Engineering from NIT Surathkal, he started his career with the Indian Navy as a commissioned officer. He later completed his Master's Program in Mechanical Engineering from IIT Kanpur and his Post Graduation Diploma Program in Management Studies from Jamnalal Bajaj Institute of Management Studies. During his 21 years of military career, he participated in three conflicts – UN Peace Keeping Mission in Somalia, Operation Parakaram (Attack on Indian Parliament), and Kargil war. The battlefield scenario taught him the importance of building trust, honesty of purpose, integrity and values. He took early retirement from the military and went on to work in the corporate sector for 8 years. While in corporate, he was fortunate to experience working in multiple areas of business i.e., Design, Marketing, Corporate Communication, Project & Business Development.

He has been actively associated with Rotary International, Indo American Chamber of Commerce (IACC), Indian Institute of Materials Management (IIMM), and Confederation of Indian Industries (CII) in various capacities. Cdr Sanjeev Raman has been lauded by Chief of Naval Staff and Commander-in-Chief for his outstanding work, while in the Navy. He is an entrepreneur by profession and a regular speaker in various forums. He lives in Jamshedpur (India), is married and blessed with a daughter.